G K Chesterton was born in London in 1874
School. He became a journalist and began w
friend Hilaire Belloc. His first novel, *The Napoleon of Notting Hill*, was published in 1904. In this book Chesterton developed his political attitudes in which he attacked socialism, big business and technology and showed how they become the enemies of freedom and justice. These were themes which were to run through his other works.

Chesterton converted to Catholicism in 1922. He explored his belief in his many religious essays and books. The best known is *Orthodoxy*, his personal spiritual odyssey.

His output was prolific. He wrote a great variety of books from biographies on Shaw and Dickens to literary criticism. He also produced poetry and many volumes of political, social and religious essays. His style is marked by vigour, puns, paradoxes and a great intelligence and personal modesty.

Chesterton is perhaps best known for his Father Brown stories. Father Brown is a modest Catholic priest who uses careful psychology to put himself in the place of the criminal in order to solve the crime.

Chesterton died in 1936.

BY THE SAME AUTHOR
ALL PUBLISHED BY HOUSE OF STRATUS

GENERAL FICTION:
THE BALL AND THE CROSS
THE MAN WHO KNEW TOO MUCH
THE NAPOLEON OF NOTTING HILL
THE PARADOXES OF MR POND
THE POET AND THE LUNATICS
THE RETURN OF DON QUIXOTE

FATHER BROWN SERIES:
THE INNOCENCE OF FATHER BROWN
THE WISDOM OF FATHER BROWN
THE INCREDULITY OF FATHER BROWN
THE SECRET OF FATHER BROWN
THE SCANDAL OF FATHER BROWN

BIOGRAPHY:
ROBERT BROWNING
CHAUCER
CHARLES DICKENS
GEORGE BERNARD SHAW
ROBERT LOUIS STEVENSON

COMMENTARY AND CRITICISM:
CRITICISMS AND APPRECIATIONS OF THE WORKS OF CHARLES DICKENS
ORTHODOXY
THE VICTORIAN AGE IN LITERATURE

G K CHESTERTON

William Blake

Copyright by the Royal Literary Fund

All rights reserved. No part of this publication may be reproduced, stored in a retrieval system, or transmitted, in any form, or by any means (electronic, mechanical, photocopying, recording, or otherwise), without the prior permission of the publisher. Any person who does any unauthorised act in relation to this publication may be liable to criminal prosecution and civil claims for damages.

The right of G K Chesterton to be identified as the author of this work has been asserted.

This edition published in 2008 by House of Stratus, an imprint of
Stratus Books Ltd., 21 Beeching Park, Kelly Bray,
Cornwall, PL17 8QS, UK.

www.houseofstratus.com

Typeset, printed and bound by House of Stratus.

A catalogue record for this book is available from the British Library and the Library of Congress.

ISBN 0-7551-165-2-6

This book is sold subject to the condition that it shall not be lent, resold, hired out, or otherwise circulated without the publisher's express prior consent in any form of binding, or cover, other than the original as herein published and without a similar condition being imposed on any subsequent purchaser, or bona fide possessor.

List of Illustrations

1   Elohim creating Adam, 1795. AKG London/Erich Lessing

2   Illustration for 'American Prophecy', 'The Terror Answered', 1793. AKG London

3   Hecate, 1795. AKG London/Erich Lessing

4   The Ancient of Days, 1793. AKG London

5   The Third Temptation. AKG London/Erich Lessing

6   Illustration for 'Jerusalem', 'Every Ornament of Perfection', 1804–20. AKG London

INTRODUCTION

William Blake would have been the first to understand that the biography of anybody ought really to begin with the words, "In the beginning God created heaven and earth." If we were telling the story of Mr Jones of Kentish Town, we should need all the centuries to explain it. We cannot comprehend even the name "Jones," until we have realised that its commonness is not the commonness of vulgar but of divine things; for its very commonness is an echo of the adoration of St John the Divine. The adjective "Kentish" is rather a mystery in that geographical connection; but the word Kentish is not so mysterious as the awful and impenetrable word "town." We shall have rent up the roots of prehistoric mankind and seen the last revolutions of modern society before we really know the meaning of the word "town." So every word we use comes to us coloured from all its adventures in history, every phase of which has made at least a faint alteration. The only right way of telling a story is to begin at the beginning – at the beginning of the world. Therefore all books have to be begun in the wrong way, for the sake of brevity. If Blake wrote the life of Blake it would not begin with any business about his birth or parentage.

Blake was born in 1757, in Carnaby Market – but Blake's life of Blake would not have begun like that. It would have begun with a great deal about the giant Albion, about the many disagreements between the spirit and the spectre of that gentleman, about the golden pillars that covered the earth at its beginning and the lions that walked in their golden innocence before God. It would have been full of symbolic wild beasts and naked women, of monstrous clouds and colossal temples; and it would all have been highly incomprehensible, but none of it would have been irrelevant. All the biggest events of Blake's life would have happened before he was born. But, on consideration, I think it will be better to tell the tale of Blake's life first and go back to his century afterwards. It is not, indeed, easy to resist temptation here, for there was much to be said about Blake before he existed. But I will resist the temptation and begin with the facts.

PART I

WILLIAM BLAKE was born on the 28th of November 1757 in Broad Street, Carnaby Market. Like so many other great English artists and poets, he was born in London. Like so many other starry philosophers and flaming mystics, he came out of a shop. His father was James Blake, a fairly prosperous hosier; and it is certainly remarkable to note how many imaginative men in our island have arisen in such an environment. Napoleon said that we English were a nation of shopkeepers; if he had pursued the problem a little further he might have discovered why we are a nation of poets. Our recent slackness in poetry and in everything else is due to the fact that we are no longer a nation of shopkeepers, but merely a nation of shop owners. In any case there seems to be no doubt that William Blake was brought up in the ordinary atmosphere of the smaller English bourgeoisie. His manners and morals were trained in the old obvious way; nobody ever thought of training his imagination, which perhaps was all the better for the neglect. There are few tales of his actual infancy. Once he lingered too long in the fields and came back to tell his mother that he had seen the prophet Ezekiel sitting under a tree. His mother smacked him. Thus ended the first adventure of William Blake in that wonderland of which he was a citizen.

His father, James Blake, was almost certainly an Irishman; his mother was probably English. Some have found in his Irish origin an explanation of his imaginative energy; the idea may be admitted, but under strong reservations. It is probably true that Ireland, if she were free from oppression, would produce more pure mystics than England. And for the same reason she would still produce fewer poets. A poet may be vague, and a mystic hates vagueness. A poet is a man who mixes up heaven and earth unconsciously. A mystic is a man who separates heaven and earth even if he enjoys them both. Broadly the English type is he who sees the elves entangled in the forests of Arcady, like Shakespeare and Keats: the Irish type is he who sees the fairies quite distinct from the forest, like Blake and Mr W B Yeats. If Blake inherited anything from his Irish blood it was his strong Irish logic. The Irish are as logical as the English are illogical. The Irish excel at the trades for which mere logic is wanted, such as law or military strategy. This element of elaborate and severe reason there certainly was in Blake. There was nothing in the least formless or drifting about him. He had a most comprehensive scheme of the universe, only that no one could comprehend it.

If Blake, then, inherited anything from Ireland it was his logic. There was perhaps in his lucid tracing of a tangled scheme of mysticism something of that faculty which enables Mr Tim Healy to understand the rules of the House of Commons. There was perhaps in the prompt pugnacity with which he kicked the impudent dragoon out of his front garden something of the success of the Irish soldier. But all such speculations are futile. For we do not know what James Blake really was, whether an Irishman by accident or by true tradition. We do not know what heredity is; the most recent investigators incline to the view that it is nothing at all. And we do not know what Ireland is; and we shall never know until Ireland is free, like any other Christian nation, to create her own institutions.

Let us pass to more positive and certain things. William Blake grew up slight and small, but with a big and very broad head, and with shoulders more broad than were natural to his stature. There exists a fine portrait of him which gives the impression of a certain squareness in the mere plan of his face and figure. He has something in common, so to speak, with the typically square men of the eighteenth century; he seems a little like Danton, without the height; like Napoleon, without the mask of Roman beauty; or like Mirabeau, without the dissipation and the disease. He had abnormally big dark eyes; but to judge by this plainly sincere portrait, the great eyes were rather bright than dark. If he suddenly entered the room (and he was likely to have entered it suddenly) I think we should have felt first a broad Bonaparte head and broad Bonaparte shoulders, and then afterwards realised that the figure under them was frail and slight.

His spiritual structure was somewhat similar, as it slowly built itself up. His character was queer but quite solid. You might call him a solid maniac or a solid liar; but you could not possibly call him a wavering hysteric or a weak dabbler in doubtful things. With his big owlish head and small fantastic figure he must have seemed more like an actual elf than any human traveller in Elfland; he was a sober native of that unnatural plain. There was nothing of the obviously fervid and futile about Blake's supernaturalism. It was not his frenzy but his coolness that was startling. From his first meeting with Ezekiel under the tree he always talked of such spirits in an everyday intonation. There was plenty of pompous supernaturalism in the eighteenth century; but Blake's was the only natural supernaturalism. Many reputable persons reported miracles; he only mentioned them. He spoke of having met Isaiah or Queen Elizabeth, not so much even as if the fact were indisputable, but rather as if so simple a thing were not worth disputing. Kings and prophets came from heaven or hell to sit to him, and he complained of them quite casually, as if they were rather troublesome professional models. He was angry because King Edward I would blunder in between him and Sir William Wallace. There have been other witnesses to the supernatural even more convincing, but I think there was never any other quite so calm. His private life, as he laid its foundations in his youth, had the same indescribable element; it was a sort of abrupt innocence. Everything that he was destined to do, especially in these early years, had a placid and prosaic oddity. He went through the ordinary fights and flirtations of boyhood; and one day he happened to be talking about the unreasonable ways of some girl to another girl. The other girl (her name was Katherine Boucher) listened with apparent patience until Blake used some phrase or mentioned some incident which (she said) she really thought was pathetic or, popularly speaking, "hard on him." "Do you?" said William Blake with great suddenness. "Then I love you." After a long pause the girl said in a leisurely manner, "I love you too." In this brief and extraordinary manner was decided a marriage of which the unbroken tenderness was tried by a long life of wild experiments and wilder opinions, and which was never truly darkened until the day when Blake, dying in an astonishing ecstasy, named her only after God.

To the same primary period of his life, boyish, romantic, and untouched, belongs the publication of his first and most famous books, "Songs of Innocence and Experience." These poems are the most natural and juvenile things Blake ever wrote. Yet they are startlingly old and unnatural poems for so young and natural a man. They have the quality already described – a matured and massive supernaturalism. If there is anything in the book extraordinary to the reader it is clearly quite ordinary to the writer. It is characteristic of him that he could write quite perfect poetry, a lyric entirely classic. No Elizabethan or Augustan could have moved with a lighter precision than –

> "O sunflower, weary of time,
> That countest the steps of the sun."

But it is also characteristic of him that he could and would put into an otherwise good poem lines like –

> "And modest Dame Lurch, who is always at church,
> Would not have handy children, nor fasting nor birch";

lines that have no sense at all and no connection with the poem whatever. There is a stronger and simpler case of contrast. There is the quiet and beautiful stanza in which Blake first described the emotions of the nurse, the spiritual mother of many children.

> "When the voices of Children are heard in the vale,
>   And laughter is heard on the hill,
> My heart is at rest within my breast
>   And everything else is still."

And here is the equally quiet verse which William Blake afterwards wrote down, equally calmly –

> "When the laughter of children is heard on the hill,
>   And whisperings are in the dale,
> The days of my youth rise fresh in my mind,
>   My face turns green and pale."

That last monstrous line is typical. He would mention with as easy an emphasis that a woman's face turned green as that the fields were green when she looked at them. That is the quality of Blake which is most personal and interesting in the fixed psychology of his youth. He came out into the world a mystic in this very practical sense, that he came out to teach rather than to learn. Even as a boy he was bursting with occult information. And all through his life he had the deficiencies of one who is always giving out and has no time to take in. He was deaf with his own cataract of speech. Hence it followed that he was devoid of patience while he was by no means devoid of charity: but impatience produced every evil effect that could practically have come from uncharitableness: impatience tripped him up and sent him sprawling twenty times in his life. The result was the unlucky paradox, that he who was always preaching perfect forgiveness seemed not to forgive even imperfectly the feeblest slights. He himself wrote in a strong epigram –

> "To forgive enemies Hayley does pretend,
> Who never in his life forgave a friend."

But the effect of the epigram is a little lost through its considerable truth if applied to the epigrammatist. The wretched Hayley had himself been a friend to Blake – and Blake could not forgive him. But this was not really lack of love or pity. It was strictly lack of patience, which in its turn was due to that bursting and almost brutal mass of convictions with which he plunged into the world like a red-hot cannon-ball, just as we have already imagined him plunging into a room with his big bullet head. His head was indeed a bullet; it was an explosive bullet.

Of his other early relations we know little. The parents who are often mentioned in his poems, both for praise and blame, are the abstract and eternal father and mother and have no individual touches. It might be inferred, perhaps, that he had a special emotional tie with his elder brother Robert, for Robert constantly appeared to him in visions and even explained to him a new method of engraving. But even this inference is doubtful, for Blake saw the oddest people in his visions, people with whom neither he nor any one else has anything particular to do; and the method of engraving might just as well have been revealed by Bubb Doddington or Prester John or the oldest baker in Brighton. That is one of the facts that makes one fancy that Blake's visions were genuine. But whoever taught him his own style of engraving, an ordinary mortal engraver taught him the ordinary mortal style, and he seems to have learnt it very well. When apprenticed by his father to a London engraving business he was diligent and capable. All his life he was a good workman, and his failures, which were many, never arose from that common idleness or looseness of life attributed to the artistic temperament. He was of a bitter and intolerant temper, but not otherwise unbusiness-like; and he was prone to insult his patrons, but not, as a rule, to fail them. But with this part of his character we shall probably have to deal afterwards. His technical skill was very great. This and a certain original touch also attracted to the young artist the attention and interest of the sculptor Flaxman.

The influence of this great man on Blake's life and work has been gravely underrated. The mistake has arisen from causes too complex to be considered, at any rate at this stage; but they resolve themselves into a misunderstanding of the nature of classicism and of the nature of mysticism. But this can be said decisively: Blake remained a Flaxmanite to the day of his death. Flaxman as a sculptor and draughtsman stood, as everybody knows, for classicism at its clearest and coldest. He would admit no line into a modern picture that might not have been on a Greek bas-relief. Even foreshortening and perspective he avoided as if there were something grotesque about them – as, indeed, there is. Nothing can be funnier, properly considered, than the fact that one's own father is a pigmy if he stands far enough off. Perspective really is the comic element in things. Flaxman vaguely felt this; Flaxman shrank from the almost insolent foreshortenings of Rubens or Veronese as he would have shrank from the gigantic boots in the foreground of an amateur photograph. For him high art was flat art in painting or drawing, everything could be done by pure line upon a single plane. Flaxman is probably best known to the existing public by his illustrations in line to Pope's "Homer," – which have certainly copied most exquisitely the austere limitations of Greek vases and reliefs. Anger may be uttered by the lifted arm or sorrow by the sunken head, but the faces of all those gods and heroes are, as you may think them, beautiful or foolish, like the faces of the dead. Above all, the line must never falter and come to nothing; Flaxman would regard a line fading away in such a picture as we should regard a railway line fading away upon a map.

This was the principle of Flaxman; and this remained to the day of his death one of the firmest principles of William Blake. I will not say that Blake took it from the great sculptor, for it formed an integral part of Blake's individual artistic philosophy; but he must have been encouraged to find it in Flaxman and strengthened in it by the influence of an older and more famous man. No one can understand Blake's pictures, no one can understand a hundred allusions in his epigrams, satires, and art criticism who does not first of all realise that William Blake was a fanatic on the subject of the firm line. The thing he loved most in art was that lucidity and decision of outline which can be seen best in the cartoons of Raphael, in the Elgin Marbles, and in the simpler designs of Michelangelo. The thing he hated most in art was the thing which we now call Impressionism – the substitution of atmosphere for shape, the sacrifice of form to tint, the cloudland of the mere colourist. With that cyclopean impudence which was the most stunning sign of his sincerity, he treated the greatest names not only as if they were despicable, but as if they were actually despised. He reasons mildly with the artistic authorities, saying –

> "You must admit that Rubens was a fool,
> And yet you make him master in your school,
> And give more money for his slobberings
> Than you will give for Raphael's finest things."

And then, with one of those sudden lunges of sense which made him a swordsman after all, he really gets home upon Rubens –

> "I understood Christ was a carpenter
> And not a brewer's drayman, my good sir."

In another satire he retells the fable of the dog, the bone, and the river, and permits (with admirable humour) the dog to expatiate upon the vast pictorial superiority of the bone's reflection in the river over the bone itself; the shadow so delicate, suggestive, rich in tone, the real bone so hard and academic in outline. He was the sharpest satirist of the Impressionists who ever wrote, only he satirised the Impressionists before they were born.

The ordinary history of Blake would obviously be that he was a man who began as a good engraver and became a great artist. The inner truth of Blake could hardly be better put than this: that he was a good artist whose idea of greatness was to be a great engraver. For him it was no mere technical accident that the art of reproduction had to cut into wood or bite into stone. He loved to think that even in being a draughtsman he was also a sculptor. When he put his lines on a decorative page he would have much preferred to carve them out of marble or cut them into rock. Like every true romantic, he loved the irrevocable. Like every true artist, he detested india-rubber. Take, for the sake of example, all the designs to the Book of Job. When he gets the thing right he gets it suddenly and perfectly right, as in the picture of all the sons of God shouting for joy. We feel that the sons of God might really shout for joy at the excellence of their own portrait. When he gets it wrong he gets it completely and incurably wrong, as in the preposterous picture of Satan dancing among paving-stones. But both are equally final and fixed. If one picture is incurably bad, the other picture is incurably good. Courage (which is, with kindness, the only fundamental virtue in man), is present and prodigious in both. No coward could have drawn such pictures.

The chief movement of Blake either in art or literature was the first publication of the batch of his own allegorical works. "The Gates of Paradise" came first, and was followed by "Urizen" and the "Book of Thel." With these he introduced his own mode of engraving and began his own style of decorative illustration. That style was steeped in the Blake and Flaxman feeling for the hard line and the harsh and heroic treatment. There were, of course, many other personalities besides that of Flaxman which were destined to influence the art of William Blake. Among others, the personality of William Blake influences it not inconsiderably. But no influence ever disturbed the love of the absolute academic line. If the reader will look at any of the designs of Blake, many of which are reproduced in this book, he will see the main fact which I mention here. Many of them are hideous, some of them are outrageous, but none of them are shapeless; none of them are what would now be called "suggestive"; none of them (in a word) are timid. The figure of man may be a monster, but he is a solid monster. The figure of God may be a mistake, but it is an unmistakable mistake. About this same time Blake began to illustrate books, decorating Blair's "Grave" and the Book of Job with his dark but very definite designs. In these plates it is quite plain that the artist, when he errs, errs not by vagueness but by hardness of treatment. The beauty of the angel upside down who blows the trumpet in the face of Blair's skeleton is the beauty of a perfect Greek athlete. And if the beauty is the beauty of an athlete, so the ugliness is the ugliness of an athlete – or perhaps of an acrobat. The contortions and clumsy attitudes of some of Blake's figures do not arise from his ignorance of the human anatomy. They arise from a sort of wild knowledge of it. He is straining muscles and cracking joints like a sportsman racing for a cup.

These book illustrations by Blake are among the simplest and strongest designs of his pencil, which at its best (to do him justice) tended to the simple and the strong. Nothing (for instance) could well be more comic or more tragic than the fact that Blake should illustrate Blair's elephantine epic called "The Grave." It was as well that Blake and Blair should meet over the grave. It was about all they had in common. The poet was full of the most crushing platitudes of eighteenth-century rationalism. The artist was full of a poetry that would have seemed frightful to the poet, a poetry inherited from the mystics of all ages and handed on to the mystics of today. Blake was the child of the Rosy Cross and the Eleusinian Mysteries; he was the father of the Pre-Raphaelite Brotherhood and even of the "Yellow Book." But of all this the excellent Mr Blair was innocent, and so, indeed, in all probability was the excellent Mr Blake. But the really interesting point is this: that the illustrations were efficient and satisfactory, from the Blair as well as the Blake point of view. The cut, for instance, with the figure of the old man bowing his head to enter the black grotto of the grave is a fine piece of drawing, apart from its meaning, and is all the finer for its simplicity. But wherever he errs it is always in being too hard and harsh, not too faint or fanciful. Blake was a greater man than Flaxman, though a less perfectly poised man. He was harder than his master, because he was madder. The figure upside down blowing the trumpet is as perfect as a Flaxman figure: only it is upside down. Flaxman upside down is almost a definition of Blake.

Such an elementary statement of Blake's idea of art is not out of place at this stage; for his convictions had formed and hardened unusually early, and his career is almost unintelligible apart from his opinions. It is fairly eccentric even with them. Flaxman had introduced him to literary society, especially to the evening parties of a Blue-stocking named Mrs Matthews. Here his force of mind was admitted; but he was not personally very popular. Most of his biographers attribute this to his "unbending deportment," and certain almost babyish candour which certainly belonged to him. But I cannot help thinking that the fact that he was in the habit of singing his own poems to tunes invented by himself may perhaps have had something to do with it. His opinions on all subjects were not only positive but aggressive. He was a fierce republican and denouncer of kings. But Mrs Matthews was probably accustomed to fierce republicans who denounced kings. She may have been less accustomed to a gentleman who insisted on wearing a red cap of liberty in ordinary society. It is due to Blake to say that his politics showed nevertheless that eccentric practicality which was mixed up with his unworldliness; it was certainly through his presence of mind that Tom Paine did not perish on the scaffold.

But Blake had none of the marks of the poetical weakling, of the mere moon-calf of mysticism. If he was a madman, one can emphasise the word man as well as the word mad. For instance, in spite of his sedentary trade and his pacific theories, he had extraordinary physical courage. Not that reasonable minimum of physical courage which is guaranteed by certain conventional sports, but intrinsic contempt of danger, a readiness to put himself into unknown perils. He would suddenly attack men much bigger and stronger than himself; and that with such violence that they were often defeated by their own amazement. He attacked a huge drayman who was harsh to some women and beat him in the most excited manner. He leapt upon a Lifeguardsman who came into his front garden, and ran that astonished warrior into the road by the elbows. The vivacity and violence of these physical outbreaks must be remembered and allowed for when we are judging some of his mental outbreaks. The most serious blot (indeed, the only serious blot) on the moral character of Blake was his habit of letting his rage get the better not only of decency but of gratitude and truth. He would abuse his benefactors as virulently as his enemies. He left epigrams lying about in which he called Flaxman a blockhead and Hayley (as far as the words can be understood) a seducer and an assassin. But the curious thing is that he often did justice to the same people both before and after such eruptions. The truth is, I fancy, that such writings were like sudden attitudes or bodily movements. We talk of a word and a blow; with Blake a word had the same momentary character as a blow. It was not a judgment, but a gesture. He had little or no feeling of the idea that "litera scripta manet." He did not see any particular reason why he should not be fond of a man merely because he had called the man a murderer a few days before. And he was innocently surprised if the man was not fond of him. In this he was perhaps rather feminine than masculine.

He had many friends and acquaintances of distinction besides Flaxman. Among them was the great Priestley, whose speculations were the life of early Unitarianism and whose Jacobin sympathies led to something not far from martyrdom; other friends were the wild optimist Godwin and his daughter Mary Woolstonecroft. But although he gained many new acquaintances he gained only one new helper. This was a Mr Thomas Butts, who lived in Fitzroy Square, and ought to have a statue there, for he is an eternal model and monument for all patrons of art. While in all other respects apparently a sane and rational British merchant, he conceived an affection for Blake's allegorical designs. But he gave no commissions for pictures; he simply gave Blake money for pictures as fast as Blake chose to paint them. The subject and size and medium were left entirely to the artist. One day Blake might leave at Fitzroy Square a little water-colour of the "Soul of a Porcupine"; the next day a gorgeous and intricate illumination in gold of the obstetrics and birth of

Cain; the next day an enormous mural painting of Hector capturing the arms of Patroclus; the following day a simple pen and ink drawing of the prophet Habbakuk taken from life. All these Mr Thomas Butts of Fitzroy Square received with solid benevolence and paid for in solid coin. Many modern writers and painters may think of such a patron somewhat dreamily. He had his reward, though it was unique rather than particularly practical. Blake regarded him with a serene affection which was never ruffled by the flying storms that were too frequent in his friendships. No allusions can be found in his poetry to the effect that Thomas Butts was a Spectre from Satan's Loins. No epigram was discovered among Blake's papers accusing Mr Butts of bereaving anybody's life. If to have kept one's own temper with Blake was a large achievement (and it was not a small one), it was certainly a truly noble achievement to have kept Blake's temper for him. And this Mr Butts and Mrs Blake can alone really claim to have done. For Blake was to pass under a patron who showed him how different is kindness from sympathy.

In the year 1800 he effected a change of residence which was in many ways an epoch in his life. He was a Londoner, though doubtless a Londoner of the time when London was small enough to feel itself on every side to be on the edge of the country. Still Blake had never in any true sense been in the heart of the country. In his earliest poems we read of seraphs stirring in the trees; but we have somehow a feeling that they were garden trees. We read of saints and sages walking in the fields, and we almost have the feeling that they were brickfields. The perfect landscape is pastoral to the point of conventionality; it has not in any sense the actual smell of England. The sights of the town are evidently as native (one might say vital) with him as any of the sights of the country. The black chimney-sweep is as obvious as the white lamb. What is worse still, time white lamb of England is no more natural or native than the alien golden lion of Africa. He was, in fact, a Cockney, like Keats; and Cockneys as a class tend to have too poetical and luxuriantly imaginative a view of life. Blake was about as little affected by environment as any man that ever lived in this world. Still he did change his environment, and it did change him.

There lived about this time near the little village of Eartham, in Sussex, a simple, kind-hearted but somewhat consequential squire of the name of Hayley. He was a landlord and an aristocrat; but he was not one of those whose vanity can be wholly fulfilled by such functions. He considered himself a patron of poetry; and indeed he was one; but, alas! he had a yet more alarming idea. He also considered himself a poet. Whether anyone agreed with that opinion while he still ruled the estates and hunted the country it is difficult now to discover. It is sufficiently certain that nobody agrees with it now. "The Triumphs of Temper," the only poem by Hayley that any modern person can remember, is probably only remembered because it was used to round off scornfully one of the ringing sentences in Macaulay's Essays. Nevertheless in his own time Hayley was a powerful and important man, quite unshaken as yet as a poet, quite unshakeable as a landed proprietor. But like almost all quite indefensible English oligarchs, he had a sort of unreasonable good nature which somehow balanced or protected his obvious unfitness and ineptitude. His heart was in the right place, though he was in the wrong one. To this blameless and beaming lord of creation, too self-satisfied to be arrogant, too solemnly childish to be cynical, too much at his ease to doubt either others or himself, to him Flaxman introduced, at him rather Flaxman threw, the red-hot cannon-ball called Blake. I wonder whether Flaxman laughed. But laughter convulses and crumples up the pure outline of the Greek profile.

Hayley, who was in his way as munificent as Maecenas (and I suspect that Maecenas was quite as stupid as Hayley), gave Blake a cottage in Felpham, a few miles from his own house, a cottage with which Blake almost literally fell in love. He writes as if he had never seen an English country cottage before; and perhaps he never had. "Nothing," he cries in a kind of ecstasy, "can ever be more grand than its simplicity and usefulness. Simple and without intricacy, it seems to be the spontaneous expression of humanity, congenial to the wants of man. No other formed house can ever please me so well." It is probably true that none ever did. All that was purest and most chivalrous in his poetry and philosophy flowered in the great winds that pass and repass between the noble Sussex hills and the sea. He was always a happy man, since he had a God. But here he was almost a contented man.

By this time had passed over Blake's head first the beginning and then the growing blackness of the great French terror. Blake was now in a world in which even he could not venture to walk about in a red cap. Moreover, like most of the menu of genius of that age and school, like Coleridge and like Shelley, he seems to have been slightly sickened with the full sensational actuality of the French tragedy; and somewhat unreasonably having urged the rebels to fight, complained because they killed people. If sincere revolutionists like Blake and Coleridge were disappointed at the Revolution, the English Government and governing class were against it with a solidity of desperation. People talk about the reign of terror in France; but allowing for the difference of national temperament and national peril, the two things were twin; there was a reign of terror in England. A gentleman was sent to penal servitude (which some gentlemen find worse than the guillotine) if he said that the Prince Regent was fat. Our terror was as cruel as Robespierre's, but more cowardly, just as our press-gang was as cruel as conscription, only more cowardly. Everywhere that the Government could knock down an enemy as if by accident, could brain a Jacobin with some brutal club of legal coincidence, the thing was done. Many such blows were struck in that time, and one of them was struck at Blake.

On a certain morning in the August of 1808 Blake walked out into his garden and found standing there a trooper of the 1st Dragoons in a scarlet coat, surveying the landscape with a satisfied air of possession. Blake expressed a desire that the dragoon should leave the garden. The dragoon expressed a desire to knock out Blake's eyes, "with many abominable imprecations." Blake sprang upon the man with startling activity, and catching him from behind by both elbows ran him out of the garden as if he were a perambulator. The man, who was probably drunk and must certainly have been surprised, went off with many verbal accusations, but none of a political nature. A little while afterwards, however, he turned up with a grave legal statement to the effect that Blake had taken the opportunity to utter these somewhat improbable words: "Damn the king, damn all his subjects, damn his soldiers, they are all slaves: when Bonaparte comes it will be cut-throat for cutthroat. I will help him." The impartial critic will be inclined to say that few persons would have even the breath to utter such political generalisations while at the same time running one of the Dragoon Guards bodily out of the gate; and it was not alleged that the incident took more than half a minute.

Blake may possibly or even probably have said "damn," but the rest of the sentence originated, I imagine, in the mind of someone else. But although most of Blake's biography treats the case as a mere clumsy accident, I can hardly think that it was so. It involves too much of a coincidence. Why did not the dragoon wander into some other garden? Why did not some other poet have to deal with the dragoon? It seems odd that the man of the red cap should be the one man to wrestle with the man of the red coat. It was a time of tyranny, and tyranny is always full of small intrigues. It is not at all impossible that the police, as we should now put it, really tried to entrap Blake. But there entered upon the scene something which in England is stronger even than the police. Hayley, not the small Hayley who was the author of the "Triumphs of Temper," but the colossal Hayley, who was the squire of Eartham and Bognor, entered the court with the extra aristocratic charm of an accident in the hunting-field. He defended Blake with generosity and good sense, such as seldom fail his class on such occasions; and Blake was acquitted. It was said that the evidence was incomplete; but I fancy that if Hayley had not come the evidence would have been complete enough.

It is unfortunate that this excellent attitude of Hayley nevertheless coincides to a great extent with the solution of the bonds that bound him to Blake. "The Visions were angry with me at Felpham," said the poet, which was his way of stating that he was somewhat bored with the benevolence of the English gentry. "Voices of celestial inhabitants were not more distinctly heard, nor their forms more distinctly seen," in the neighbourhood of the Squire of

Eartham than in that of Mr Butts of Fitzroy Square; and Blake abruptly returned to London, taking lodgings just off Oxford Street. He started at once on a work with the promising title, "Jerusalem, the Emanation of the Giant Albion." I say there is a certain pathos in this parting from Hayley, for he was now to fall into the power of a much more unpleasant kind of capitalist. Poor Blake fell indeed from bad to worse in the matter of patrons. Butts was sensible and sympathetic, Hayley was honest and silly. And his last protector seems to have been something very like a swindler.

The name of this benevolent being was Richard Hartley Cromek, a Yorkshireman, and a publisher. He found Blake in bitter poverty after his breach with Hayley (he and his wife lived on 10s a week), and his method of sweating was of the simplest and most artistic character. He used to go to Blake, tell him that he would give him the engraving of a number of designs; he would easily make Blake talk enthusiastically, show his sketches and so on; then having got the sketches he would go away and give the engraving to somebody else. This annoyed Blake. It is pleasant to reflect that it was about Cromek that the best of his epigrams was written –

> "A petty sneaking knave I knew…
> Oh, Mr Cromek, how do you do?"

Blake's irritation broke out, as was common with him, not over the clearest but over the most confused case of Cromek's misconduct. The publisher had seen a design by Blake of Chaucer's "Canterbury Pilgrims," and commissioned Blake to complete it. A few days afterwards Cromek found himself in the studio of the popular painter Stothard, and suggested the subject to him. Stothard finished his picture first and it appeared before Blake's. Blake went into one of his worst rages and wrote one of his best pieces of prose.

A brother artist said of Blake, with beautiful simplicity, "He is a good man to steal from." The remark is as philosophical as it is practical. Blake had the great mark of real intellectual wealth; anything that fell from him might be worth picking up. What he dropped in the street might as easily be half-a-sovereign as a halfpenny. Moreover, he invited theft in this further sense, that his mental wealth existed, so to speak, in the most concentrated form. It is easier to steal half-a-sovereign in gold than in halfpence. He was literally packed with ideas – with ideas which required unpacking. In him and his works they were too compressed to be intelligible; they were too brief to be even witty. And as a thief might steal a diamond and turn it into twenty farms, so the plagiarist of Blake might steal a sentence and turn it into twenty volumes. It was profitable to steal an epigram from Blake for three reasons –

first, that the original phrase was small and would not leave a large gap; second, that it was cosmic and synthetic and could be applied to things in general; third, that it was unintelligible and no one would know it again. I could give innumerable instances of what I mean; I will let one instance stand for the rest. In the middle of that long poem which is so disconnected that it may reasonably be doubted whether it is a long poem at all (I mean that commonly bearing the title "The Auguries of Innocence"), he introduces these two lines:

> "When gold and gems adorn the plough
> To peaceful arts shall envy bow."

A careless and honest man would read these lines and make nothing of them. A careful thief might make out of them a whole entertaining and symbolic romance, like " Gulliver's Travels" or "Erywhon." The idea obviously is this; – that we still for some reason admit the tools of destruction to be nobler than the tools of production, because decorative art is expended on the one and not on the other. The sword has a golden hilt; but no plough has golden handles. There is such a thing as a sword of state; there is no such thing as a scythe of state. Men come to court wearing imitation swords; few men come to court wearing imitation flails. It is fascinating to reflect how fantastic a story might be written upon this hint by Blake. But Blake does not write the story; he only gives the hint, and that so hurriedly that even as a hint it may hardly be understood.

Most of Blake's quarrels were trivial, and some were little short of discreditable. But in his quarrel with Cromek and Stothard he does really stand as the champion of all that is heroic and ideal, as against all that is worldly and insincere. The celebrated Stothard was at this time in the height of his earlier success; he occupied somewhat the same relation to art and society that has been occupied within our own time by Frederic Leighton. He was, like Leighton, an accomplished draughtsman, a man of slight but genuine poetic feeling, an artist who thoroughly realised that the aim of art was to please. Ruskin said of him very truly (I forget the exact words) that there were no thorns to his roses. At the same time, his smoothness was a smoothness of innocence rather than a smoothness of self-indulgence; his work has a girlish timidity rather than any real conventional cowardice; he was a true artist in a somewhat effeminate style of art. Nor is there any reason to doubt that his personal character was as clean and good natured as his pictures. It may be that he began his *Canterbury Pilgrims* without any commission from Cromek, or it may be that he took the commission from Cromek without the least idea that the conception had been borrowed from Blake. That Cromek treated Blake badly is beyond dispute; that Stothard treated him badly is unproved; but Blake was not much in the habit of waiting for proof in such cases. Stothard, I say, may not have been morally in the wrong at all. But he was intellectually and critically very much in the wrong; and Blake pointed this out in a pamphlet which, though defaced here and there with his fantastic malice, is a solid and powerful contribution to artistic and literary criticism.

Stothard, the elegant gentleman, the man of sensibility, the eighteenth-century aesthete, cast his condescending eye upon the Middle Ages. He was of that age and school that only saw the Middle Ages by moonlight. Chaucer's Pilgrims were to him a quaint masquerade of hypocrisy or superstition, now only interesting from its comic or antiquated costume. The monk was amusing because he was fat, the wife of Bath because she was gay, the Squire because he was dandified, and so on. Blake knew as little about the Middle Ages as Stothard did; but Blake knew about eternity and about man; he saw the image of God under all garments. And in a rage which may really be called noble he tore in pieces Stothard's antiquarian frivolity, and asked him to look with a more decent reverence at the great creations of a great poet. Stothard called the young Squire of Chaucer "a fop." Blake points out forcibly and with fine critical truth that the daintiness of the Squire's dress is the mere last touch to his youth, gaiety, and completeness; but that he was no fop at all, but a serious, chivalrous, and many-sided gentleman who enjoyed books, understood music, and was hardy and prompt in battle. Moreover, he is definitely described as humble, reverent, and full of filial respect. That such a man should be called a fop because of a frill or a feather Blake rightly regarded as a sign of the mean superficiality of his rival's ideas. Stothard spoke of "the fair young wife of Bath"; Blake placidly points out that she had had four husbands, and was, as in Blake's picture, a loud, lewd, brazen woman of quite advanced age, but of enormous vitality and humour. Stothard makes the monk the mere comic monk of commonplace pictures, shaped like a wine barrel and as full of wine. Blake points out that Chaucer's monk was a man, and an influential man; not without sensual faults, but also not without dignity and authority. Everywhere, in fact, he reminds his opponent that in entering the world of Chaucer he is not entering a fancy-dress ball, but a temple carved with colossal and eternal images of the gods of good and evil. Stothard was only interested in Chaucer's types because they were dead; Blake was interested in them because they cannot die. In many of Blake's pictures may be found one figure quite monotonously recurrent – the figure of a monstrously muscular old man, with hair and beard like a snowstorm, but with limbs like young trees. That is Blake's root conception; the Ancient of Days; the thing which is old with all the awfulness of its past, but young with all the energies of its future.

I make no excuse for dwelling at length on this in a life of Blake; it is the most important event. It is worth while to describe this quarrel between Blake and Stothard, because it is really a symbolic quarrel, interesting to the whole world of artists and important to the whole destiny of art. It is the quarrel between the artist who is a poet and the artist who is only a painter. In many of his merely technical designs Blake was a better and bolder artist than Stothard; still, I should admit, and most people who saw the two pictures would be ready to admit, that Stothard's *Canterbury Pilgrims* as a mere piece of drawing and painting is better than Blake's. But this if anything only makes the whole argument more certain. It is the duel between the artist who wishes only to be an artist and the artist who has the higher and harder ambition to be a man – that is, an archangel. Or, again, it might be put thus: whether an artist ought to be a universalist or whether he is better as a specialist. Now against the specialist, against the man who studies only art or electricity, or the violin, or the thumbscrew or what not, there is only one really important argument, and that, for some reason or other, is never offered. People say that specialists are inhuman; but that is unjust. People say an expert is not a man; but that is unkind and untrue. The real difficulty about the specialist or expert is much more singular and fascinating. The trouble with the expert is never that he is not a man; it is always that wherever he is not an expert he is too much of an ordinary man. Wherever he is not exceptionally learned he is quite casually ignorant. This is the great fallacy in the case of what is called the impartiality of men of science. If scientific men had no idea beyond their scientific work it might be all very well – that is to say, all very well for everybody except them. But the truth is that, beyond their scientific ideas, they have not the absence of ideas but the presence of the most vulgar and sentimental ideas that happen to be common to their social clique. If a biologist had no views on art and morals it might be all very well. The truth is that a biologist has all the wrong views of art and morals that happen to be going about in the smart set in his time. If Professor Tyndall had held no views about politics, he could have done no harm with his views about evolution. Unfortunately, however, he held a very low order of political ideas from his sectarian and Orange ancestry; and those ideas have poisoned evolution to this day. In short, the danger of the mere technical artist or expert is that of becoming a snob or average silly man in all things not affecting his peculiar topic of study; wherever he is not an extraordinary man he is a particularly stupid ordinary man. The very fact that he has studied machine guns to fight the French proves that he has not studied the French. Therefore he will probably say that they eat frogs. The very fact that he has learnt to paint the light on medieval armour proves that he has not studied the medieval philosophy. Therefore he will probably suppose that medieval barons did nothing but order vassals into the dungeons beneath the castle moat. Now all through the eighteenth and early nineteenth centuries art, that is, the art of painting, suffered terribly from this conventional and uncultured quality in the working artist. People talk about something pedantic in the knowledge of the expert; but what ruins mankind is the ignorance of the expert. In the period of which we speak the experts in painting were bursting with this ignorance. The early essays of Thackeray are full of the complaint, that the whole trouble with painters was that they only knew how to paint. If they had painted unimportant or contemptible subjects, all would have been well; if they had painted the nearest donkey or lamp-post no one would have complained. But exactly because they were experts they fell into the mere snobbish sentimentalism of their times; they insisted on painting all the things they had read about in the cheapest history books and the most maudlin novels. As Thackeray has immortally described in the case of Mr Gandish, they painted Boadishia and declared that they had discovered "in their researches into 'istry" the story of King Alfred and the Cakes. In other words, the expert does not escape his age; he only lays himself open to the meanest and most obvious of the influences of his age. The specialist does not avoid having prejudices; he only succeeds in specialising in the most passing and illiterate prejudices.

Of all this type of technical ignorance Stothard is absolutely typical. He was an admirable instance of the highly cultivated and utterly ignorant man. He had spent his life in making lines swerve smoothly and shadows creep exactly into their right place; he had never had any time to understand the things that he was drawing except by their basest and most conventional connotation. Somebody suggested that he should draw some medieval pilgrims – that is, some vigorous types in the heyday of European civilisation in the act of accepting the European religion. But he who alone could draw them right was especially likely to see them wrong. He had learnt, like a modern, the truth from newspapers, because he had no time to read even encyclopaedias. He had learnt how to paint armour and armorial bearings; it was too much to expect him to understand them. He had learnt to draw a horse; it was too late to ask him to ride one. His whole business was somehow or other to make pictures; and therefore when he looked at Chaucer, he could see nothing but the picturesque.

Against this sort of sound technical artist, another type of artist has been eternally offered; this was the type of Blake. It was also the type of Michelangelo; it was the type of Leonardo de Vinci; it was the type of several French mystics, and in our own country and recent period, of Rossetti. Blake, as a painter among other things, belongs to that small group of painters who did something else besides paint. But this is indeed a very inadequate way of stating the matter. The fuller and fairer way is this: that Blake was one of those few painters who understood his subject as well as his picture. I have already said that I think Stothard's picture of the *Canterbury Pilgrims* in a purely technical sense better than his. Indeed, there is nothing to be said against

Stothard's picture of the Canterbury Pilgrims, except that it is not a picture of the *Canterbury Pilgrims*. Blake (to summarise the whole matter as simply as it can be summarised) was in the tradition of the best and most educated ideas about Chaucer; Stothard was the inheritor of the most fashionable ideas and the worst. The whole incident cannot be without its moral and effect for all discussions about the morality or unmorality of art. If art could be unmoral it might be all very well. But the truth is that unless art is moral, art is not only immoral, but immoral in the most commonplace, slangy, and prosaic way. In the future, the fastidious artists who refuse to be anything but artists will go down to history as the embodiment of all the vulgarities and banalities of their time. People will point to a picture by Mr Sargent or Mr Shannon and say, "See, that man had caught all the most middle class cant of the early twentieth century."

We can now recur, however, to the general relations of Blake with his later patron. In a phrase of singular unconscious humour Mr Cromek accused Blake of "a want of common politeness." Common politeness certainly can hardly be said to have been Blake's strong point. But Cromek's politeness was certainly an uncommon sort of politeness. One is tempted to be thankful that it is not a common sort. Cromek's notion of common politeness was to give the artist a guinea a drawing on the understanding that he should get some more for engraving them, and then give the engraving to somebody else who cost him next to nothing. Blake, as we have said, resented this startling simplicity of swindling. Blake was in such matters a singular mixture of madness and shrewdness in the judgment of such things. He was the kind of man whom a publisher found at one moment more vague and viewless than any poet, and at the next moment more prompt and rapacious than any literary agent. He was sometimes above his commercial enemy, sometimes below him; but he never was on his level; one never knew where he was. Cromek's letter is a human document of extraordinary sincerity and interest. The Yorkshire publisher positively breaks for once in his life into a kind of poetry. He describes Blake as being "a combination of the serpent and the dove." He did not quite realise, perhaps, that according to the New Testament he was paying Blake a compliment. But the truth is, I fancy, that the painter and poet had been one too many for the publisher. I think that on any occasion Cromek would have willingly forgiven Blake for showing the harmlessness of the dove. I fancy that on one occasion Blake must have shown the wisdom of the serpent.

From the mere slavery of this sweater Blake was probably delivered by the help of the last and most human of his patrons, a young man named John Linnell, a landscape painter and a friend of the great Mulready. It is extraordinary to think that he was young enough to die in 1882; and that a man who had read in the Prophetic Books the last crusades of Blake may have lived to read in the newspapers some of the last crusades of Gladstone. This man Linnell covers the last years of Blake as with an ambulance tent in the wilderness. Blake never had any ugly relations with Linnell, just as he had never had any with Butts. His quarrels had wearied many friends; but by this time I think he was too weary even to quarrel. On Linnell's commission he began a system of illustrations to Dante; but I think that no one expected him to live to finish it.

His last sickness fell upon him very slowly, and he does not seem to have taken much notice of it. He continued perpetually his pictorial designs; and as long as they were growing stronger he seems to have cared very little for the fact that he was growing weaker himself. One of the last designs he made was one of the strongest he ever made – the tremendous image of the Almighty bending forward, foreshortened in a colossal perspective, to trace out the heavens with a compass. Nowhere else has he so well expressed his primary theistic ideas – that God, though infinitely gigantic, should be as solid as a giant. He had often drawn men from the life; not unfrequently he had drawn his dead men from the life. Here, according to his own conceptions, he may be said to have drawn God from the life. When he had finished the portrait (which he made sitting up in his sick-bed) he called out cheerfully, "What shall I draw after that?" Doubtless he racked his brain for some superlative spirit or archangel which would not be a mere bathos after the other. His rolling eyes (those round lustrous eyes which one can always see roll in his painted portraits) fell on the old frail and somewhat ugly woman who had been his companion so long, and he called out, "Catherine, you have been an angel to me; I will draw you next." Throwing aside the sketch of God measuring the universe, he began industriously to draw a portrait of his wife, a portrait which is unfortunately lost, but which must have substantially resembled the remarkable sketch which a friend drew some months afterwards; the portrait of a woman at once plain and distinguished, with a face that is supremely humorous and at once harsh and kind. Long before that portrait was drawn, long before those months had elapsed, William Blake was dead.

Whatever be the explanation, it is quite certain that Blake had more positive joy on his death-bed than any other of the sons of Adam. One has heard of men singing hymns on their death-beds, in low plaintive voices. Blake was not at all like that on his death-bed: the room shook with his singing. All his songs were in praise of God, and apparently new: all his songs were songs of innocence. Every now and then he would stop and cry out to his wife, "Not mine! Not mine!" in a sort of ecstatic explanation. He truly seemed to wait for the opening of the door of death as a child waits for the opening of the cupboard on his birthday. He genuinely and solemnly seemed to hear the hoofs of the horses of death as a baby hears on Christmas eve the reindeer-hooves of Santa Claus. He was in his last moments in that wonderful world of whiteness in which white is still a colour. He would have clapped his hands at a white snowflake and sung as at the white wings of an angel at the moment when he himself turned suddenly white with death.

And now, after a due pause, someone will ask and we must answer a popular question which, like many popular questions, is really a somewhat deep and subtle one. To put the matter quite simply, as the popular instinct would put it, "Was William Blake mad?" It is easy enough to say, of course, in the non-committal modern manner that it all depends on how you define madness. If you mean it in its practical or legal sense (which is perhaps the most really useful sense of all), if you mean was William Blake unfit to look after himself, unable to exercise civic functions or to administer property, then certainly the answer is "No." Blake was a citizen, and capable of being a very good citizen. Blake, so far from being incapable of managing property, was capable (in so far as he chose) of collecting a great deal of it. His conduct was generally business-like; and when it was unbusiness-like it was not through any subhuman imbecility or superhuman abstraction, but generally through an unmixed exhibition of very human bad temper. Again, if when we say "Was Blake mad?" we mean was he fundamentally morbid, was his soul cut off from the universe and merely feeding on itself, then again the answer is emphatically "No." There was nothing defective about Blake; he was in contact with all the songs and smells of the universe, and he was entirely guiltless of that one evil element which is almost universal in the character of the morbidly insane – I mean secrecy. Yet again, if we mean by madness anything inconsistent or unreasonable, then Blake was not mad. Blake was one of the most consistent men that ever lived, both in theory and practice. Blake may have been quite wrong, but he was not in the least unreasonable. He was quite as calm and scientific as Herbert Spencer on the basis of his own theory of things. He was vain to the last degree; but it was the gay and gusty vanity of a child, not the imprisoned pride of a maniac. In all these aspects we can say with confidence that the man was not at least obviously mad or completely mad. But if we ask whether there was not some madness about him, whether his naturally just mind was not subject to some kind of disturbing influence which was not essential to itself, then we ask a very different question, and require, unless I am mistaken, a very different answer.

When all Philistine mistakes are set aside, when all mystical ideas are appreciated, there is a real sense in which Blake was mad. It is a practical and certain sense, exactly like the sense in which he was not mad. In fact, in almost every case of his character and extraordinary career we can safely offer this proposition, that if there was something wrong with it, it was wrong even from his own best standpoint. People talk of appealing from Philip drunk to Philip sober; it is easy to appeal from Blake mad to Blake sane.

When Blake lived at Felpham angels appear to have been as native to the Sussex trees as birds. Hebrew patriarchs walked on the Sussex Downs as easily as if they were in the desert. Some people will be quite satisfied with saying that the mere solemn attestation of such miracles marks a man as a madman or a liar. But that is a short cut of sceptical dogmatism which is not far removed from impudence. Surely we cannot take an open question like the supernatural and shut it with a bang, turning the key of the mad-house on all the mystics of history. To call a man mad because he has seen ghosts is in a literal sense religious persecution. It is denying him his full dignity as a citizen because he cannot be fitted into your theory of the cosmos. It is disfranchising him because of his religion. It is just as intolerant to tell an old woman that she cannot be a witch as to tell her that she must be a witch. In both cases you are setting your own theory of things inexorably against the sincerity or sanity of human testimony. Such dogmatism at least must be quite as impossible to anyone calling himself an agnostic as to anyone calling himself a spiritualist. You cannot take the region called the unknown and calmly say that though you know nothing about it, you know that all its gates are locked. You cannot say, "This island is not discovered yet; but I am sure that it has a wall of cliffs all round it and no harbour." That was the whole fallacy of Herbert Spencer and Huxley when they talked about the unknowable instead of about the unknown. An agnostic like Huxley must concede the possibility of a gnostic like Blake. We do not know enough about the unknown to know that it is unknowable.

If, then, people call Blake mad merely for seeing ghosts and angels, we shall venture to dismiss them as highly respectable but very bigoted people. But then, again, there is another line along which the same swift assumption can be made. While he was at Felpham Blake's eccentricity broke out on another side. A quality that can frankly be called indecency appeared in his pictures, his opinions, and to some extent in his conduct. But it was an idealistic indecency. Blake's mistake was not so much that he aimed at sin as that he aimed at – an impossible and inhuman sinlessness. It is said that he proposed to his wife that they should live naked in their back garden like Adam and Eve. If the husband ever really proposed this, the wife succeeded in averting it. But in his verse and prose, particularly in some of the Prophetic Books, he began to talk very wildly. However far he really meant to go against common morality, he certainly meant (like Walt Whitman) to go the whole way against common decency. He professed to regard the veiling of the most central of human relations as the unnatural cloaking of a natural work. He was never at a loss for an effective phrase; and in one of his poems on this topic he says finely if fallaciously –

> "Does the sower sow by night
> Or the ploughman in darkness plough?"

But his speculations went past decorum and at least touched the idea of primary law. In some parts of the Prophetic Books (written in the period which may fairly be called a paroxysm) he really seems to be preaching the idea that sin is sometimes a good thing because it leads to forgiveness. I cannot think this idea does much credit to Blake's power of logic, which was generally good. The very fact of forgiveness implies that what led up to it was evil. But though the position is hardly rational, it is quite unfair to say that it is insane. It is no sillier or more untenable than a hundred sophistries that one may hear at every tea-table or read in every magazine. A little while ago the family of a young lady attempted to shut her up in an asylum because she believed in Free Love. This atrocious injustice was stopped; but many people wrote to the papers to say that marriage was a very fine thing – as indeed it is. Of course the answer was simple: that if everyone with silly opinions were locked up in an asylum, the asylums of the twentieth century would have to be somewhat unduly enlarged. The same common-sense applies to the case of Blake. That he did maintain some monstrous propositions proves that he was not always right, that he had even a fine faculty for being exceedingly wrong. But it does not prove that he was a madman or anything remotely resembling one. Nor is there any reason to suppose that he was carried into any practice inconsistent with his strong domestic affections. Indeed, I think that much of Blake's anarchy is connected with his innocence. I have noticed the combination more than once, especially in men of Irish blood like Blake. Heavy, full-blooded men feel the need of bonds and are glad to bind themselves. But the chaste are often lawless. They are theoretically reckless, because they are practically pure. Thus Ireland, while it is the island of rebels is also the island of saints, and might be called the island of virgins.

But when we have reached this point – that this ugly element in Blake was an intrusion of Blake's mere theory of things – we have come, I think, very close to the true principle to be pursued in estimating his madness or his sanity. Blake the mere poet, would have been decent and respectable. It was Blake the logician who was forced to be almost blackguardly. In other words, Blake was not mad; for such part of him as was mad was not Blake. It was an alien influence, and in a sense even an accidental one; in an extreme sense it might even be called antagonist. Properly to appreciate what this influence was, we must see the man's artistic character as a whole and notice what are its biggest forces and its biggest defects when taken in the bulk – in the whole mass of his poetry, his pictures, his criticism and his conversation. Blake's position can be summed up as a sufficiently simple problem. Blake could do so many things. Why is it that he could do none of them quite right?

Blake was not a frail or fairy-like sort of person; he had not the light unity, the capering completeness of the entirely irresponsible man. He had not the independence, one might almost say the omnipotence, that comes from being hopelessly weak. There was nothing in him of Mr Skimpole; he was not a puff of silver thistledown. He was not a reed shaken in the wind in Jordan. He was rather an oak rooted in England, but an oak half killed by the ivy. The interesting question of spiritual botany is – What was the ivy that half killed him? Originally his intellect was not only strong but strongly rational – one might almost say strongly sceptical. There never was a man of whom it was less true to say (as has been said) that he was a light sensitive lyrist, a mere piper of pretty songs for children. His mind was like a ruined Roman arch; it has been broken by barbarians; but what there is of it is Roman. So it was with William Blake's reason; it had been broken (or cracked) by something; but what there was of it was reasonable. in his art criticism he never said anything that was not strictly consistent with his first principles. In his controversies, in the many matters in which he argued angrily or venomously, he never lost the thread of the argument. Like every great mystic he was also a great rationalist. Read Blake's attack upon Stothard's picture of the *Canterbury Pilgrims*, and you will see that he could not only write a quite sensible piece of criticism, but even a quite slashing piece of journalism. By nature one almost feels that he might have done anything; have conducted campaigns like Napoleon or studied the stars like Newton. But something, when all is said and done, had eaten away whole parts of that powerful brain, leaving parts of it standing like great Greek pillars in a desert. What was this thing?

MADNESS is not an anarchy. Madness is a bondage: a contraction. I will not call Blake mad because of anything he would say. But I will call him mad in so far as there was anything he *must* say. Now, there are notes of this tyranny in Blake. It was not like the actual disease of the mind that makes a man believe he is a cat or a dog; it was more like the disease of the nerves, which makes a man say "dog" when he means "cat." One mental jump or jerk of this nature may be especially remarked in Blake. He had in his poetry one very peculiar habit, a habit which cannot be considered quite sane. It was the habit of being haunted, one may say hag-ridden by a fixed phrase, which gets itself written in ten separate poems on quite different subjects, when it had no apparent connection with any of them. The amusing thing is that the omnipresent piece of poetry is generally the one piece that is quite incomprehensible. The verse that Blake's readers can understand least seems always to be the verse that Blake likes best. I give an ordinary instance, if anything connected with Blake can be called ordinary.

The harmless Hayley, who was a fool, but a gentleman and a poet (a country gentleman and a very minor poet), provoked Blake's indignation by giving him commissions for miniatures when he wanted to do something else, probably frescoes as big as the house. Blake wrote the epigram –

> "If Hayley knows the thing you cannot do,
> That is the very thing he'll set you to."

And then, feeling that there was a lack of colour and warmth in the portrait, he lightly added, for no reason in particular, the lines –

> "And when he could not act upon my wife,
> Hired a villain to bereave my life."

There is, apparently, no trace here of any allusion to fact. Hayley never tried to bereave anybody's life. He lacked even the adequate energy. Nevertheless I should not say for a moment that this startling fiction proved Blake to be mad. It proved him to be violent and recklessly suspicious; but there was never the least doubt that he was that. But now turn to another poem of Blake's, a merely romantic and narrative poem called "Fair Eleanor," which is all about somebody acting on somebody else's wife. Here we find the same line repeated word for word in quite another connection –

> "Hired a villain to bereave my life."

It is not a musical line; it does not resemble English grammar to any great extent. Yet Blake is somehow forced to put it into a poem about a real person exactly as he had put it into an utterly different poem about a fictitious person. There seems no particular reason for writing it even once; but he has to write it again and again. This is what I do call a mad spot on the mind. I should not call Blake mad for hating Hayley or for boiling Hayley (though he had done him nothing but kindness), or for making up any statements however monstrous or mystical about Hayley. I should not in the least degree think that Blake was mad if he had said that he saw Hayley's soul in hell, that it had green hair, one eye, and a serpent for a nose. A man may have a wild vision without being insane; a man may have a lying vision without being insane. But I should smell insanity if in turning over Blake's books I found that this one pictorial image obsessed him apart from its spiritual meaning; if I found that the arms of the Black Prince in "King Edward III." were a cyclops vert rampant, nosed serpentine; if I found that Flaxman was praised for his kindness to a one eyed animal with green bristles and a snaky snout; if Albion or Ezekiel had appeared to Blake and commanded him to write a history of the men in the moon, who are one-eyed, green-haired, with long curling noses; if any flimsy sketch or fine decorative pattern that came from Blake's pencil might reproduce ceaselessly and meaninglessly the writhing proboscis and the cyclopean eye. I should call that morbidity or even madness; for it would be the triumph of the palpable image over its own intellectual meaning. And there is something of *that* madness in the dark obstinacy or weakness that makes Blake introduce again and again these senseless scraps of rhyme, as if they were spells to keep off the devil.

In four of five different poems, without any apparent connection with those poems, occur these two extraordinary lines –

"The caterpillar on the leaf
Repeats to thee thy mother's grief."

In the abstract this might perhaps mean something, though it would, I think, take most people some time to see what it could mean. In the abstract it may perhaps involve some allusion to a universal law of sacrifice in nature. In the concrete – that is, in the context – it involves no allusion to anything in heaven or earth. Here is another couplet that constantly recurs –

"The red blood ran from the grey monk's side,
His hands and his feet were wounded wide."

This is worse still; for this cannot be merely abstract. The ordinary rational reader will naturally exclaim at last, with a not unnatural explosion, "Who the devil is the grey monk? and why should he be always bleeding in places where he has no business?" Now to say that this sort of thing is not insanity of some kind is simply to play the fool with the words. A madman who writes this may be higher than ordinary humanity; so may any madman in Hanwell. But he is a madman in every sense that the word has among men. I have taken this case of actual and abrupt irrelevance as the strongest form of the thing; but it has other forms almost equally decisive. For instance, Blake had a strong sense of humour, but it was not under control; it could be eclipsed and could completely disappear. There was certainly a spouting fountain of fierce laughter in the man who could write in an epigram –

"A dirty sneaking knave I knew...

Oh, Mr Cromek, how do you do?"

Yet the laughter was as fitful as it was fierce; and it can suddenly fail. Blake's sense of humour can sometimes completely desert him. He writes a string of verses against cruelty to the smallest creature as a sort of mystical insult to the universe. It contains such really fine couplets as these –

> "Each outcry of the hunted hare
> A fibre from the brain can tear."

> "A skylark wounded in the wing,
> A cherubim does cease to sing."

Or again, in a more fanciful but genuinely weird way –

> "He who torments the chafer's sprite
> Weaves a bower in endless night."

And then, after all this excellent and quite serious poetry, Blake can calmly write down the following two lines –

> "He who the ox to wrath has moved
> Shall never be by woman loved."

One could hardly find a more Gilbertian absurdity in the conjunction of ideas in the whole of the "Bab Ballads" than the idea that the success of some gentleman in the society of ladies depends upon whether he has previously at some time or other slightly irritated an ox. Such sudden inaccessibility to laughter must be called a morbid symptom. It must mean a blind spot on the brain. The whole thing, of course, would prove nothing if Blake were a common ranter incapable of writing well, or a common dunce incapable of seeing a joke. Such a man might easily be sane enough; he might be as sane as he was stupid. If Blake had always written badly he might be sane. But a man who could write so well and did write so badly must be mad.

What was it that was eating away a part of Blake's brain? I venture to offer an answer which in the eyes of many people will have nothing to recommend it except the accident of its personal sincerity. I firmly believe that what did hurt Blake's brain was the reality of his spiritual communications. In the case of all poets, and especially in the case of Blake, the phrase "an inspired poet" commonly means a good poet. About Blake it is specially instinctive. And about Blake, I am quite convinced, it is specially untrue. His inspired poems were not his good poems. His inspired poems were very often his particularly bad ones; they were bad by inspiration. If a ploughman says that he saw a ghost, it is not quite sufficient to answer merely that he is a madman. It may have been seeing the ghost that drove him mad. His lunacy may not prove the falsehood of his tale, but rather its terrible truth. So in the same way I differ from the common or sceptical critics of a man like Blake. Such critics say that his visions were false because he was mad. I say he was mad because his visions were true. It was exactly because he was unnaturally exposed to a hail of forces that were more than natural that some breaches were made in his mental continuity, some damage was done to his mind. He was, in a far more awful sense than Goldsmith, "an inspired idiot." He was an idiot because he was inspired.

When he said of "Jerusalem" that its authors were in eternity, one can only say that nobody is likely to go there to get any more of their work. He did not say that the author of "The Tyger" was in eternity; the author of that glorious thing was in Carnaby Market. It will generally be found, I think, with some important exceptions, that whenever Blake talked most about inspiration he was actually least inspired. That is, he was least inspired by whatever spirit presides over good poetry and good thinking. He was abundantly inspired by whatever spirit presides over bad poetry or bad thinking. Whatever god specialises in unreadable and almost unpronounceable verse was certainly present when he invented the extraordinary history of "William Bond" or the maddening metre of the lines "To Mr Butts." Whatever archangel rules over utter intellectual error had certainly spread his wings of darkness over Blake when he came to the conclusion that a man ought to be bad in order to be pardoned. But these unthinkable thoughts are mostly to be found in his most unliterary productions; notably in the Prophetic Books. To put my meaning broadly, the opinions which nobody can agree with are mostly in the books that nobody can read. I really believe that this was not from Blake, but from his spirits. It is all very well for great men, like Mr Rossetti and Mr Swinburne, to trust utterly to the seraphim of Blake. They may naturally trust angels – they do not believe in them. But I do believe in angels, and incidentally in fallen angels.

There is no danger to health in being a mystic; but there may be some danger to health in being a spiritualist. It would be a very poor pun to say that a taste for spirits is bad for the health; nevertheless, oddly enough, though a poor pun it is a perfectly correct philosophical parallel. The difference between having a real religion and having a mere curiosity about psychic marvels is really very like the difference between drinking beer and drinking brandy, between drinking wine and drinking gin. Beer is a food as well as a stimulant; so a positive religion is a comfort as well as an adventure.

A man drinks his wine because it is his favourite wine, the pleasure of his palate or the vintage of his valley. A man drinks alcohol merely because it is alcoholic. So a man calls upon his gods because they are good or at any rate good to him, because they are the idols that protect his tribe or the saints that have blessed his birthday. But spiritualists call upon spirits merely because they are spirits; they ask for ghosts merely because they are ghosts. I have often been haunted with a fancy that the creeds of men might be paralleled and represented in their beverages. Wine might stand for genuine Catholicism and ale for genuine Protestantism; for these at least are real religions with comfort and strength in them. Clean cold Agnosticism would be clean cold water, an excellent thing, if you can get it. Most modern ethical and idealistic movements might be well represented by soda-water – which is a fuss about nothing. Mr Bernard Shaw's philosophy is exactly like black coffee – it awakens but it does not really inspire. Modern hygienic materialism is very like cocoa; it would be impossible to express one's contempt for it in stronger terms than that. Sometimes, very rarely, one may come across something that may honestly be compared to milk, an ancient and heathen mildness, an earthly yet sustaining mercy – the milk of human kindness. You can find it in a few pagan poets and a few old fables; but it is everywhere dying out. Now if we adopt this analogy for the sake of argument, we shall really come back to the bad pun; we shall conclude that a taste for spiritualism is very like a taste for spirits. The man who drinks gin or methylated spirit does it only because it makes him super-normal; so the man who with tables or planchettes invokes supernatural beings invokes them only because they are supernatural. He does not know that they are good or wise or helpful. He knows that he desires the deity, but he does not even know that he likes him. He attempts to invoke the god without adoring him. He is interested in whatever he can find out touching supernatural existence; but he is not really filled with joy as by the face of a divine friend, any more than anyone actually likes the taste of methylated spirit. In such psychic investigations, in a word, there is excitement, but not affectional satisfaction; there is brandy, but no food.

Now Blake was in the most reckless, and sometimes even in the most vulgar, sense a spiritualist. He threw the doors of his mind open to what the late George Macdonald called in a fine phrase "the canaille of the other world." I think it is impossible to look at some of the pictures which Blake drew, under what he considered direct spiritual dictation, without feeling that he was from time to time under influences that were not only evil but even foolishly evil. I give one case out of numberless cases. Blake drew, from his own vision a head which he called *The Man who built the Pyramids*. Anyone can appreciate the size and mystery of the idea; and most people would form some sort of fancy of how a great poetical painter, such as Michelangelo or Watts, would have rendered the idea; they can conceive a face swarthy and secret, or ponderous and lowering, or staring and tropical, or Appolonian and pure. Whatever was the man who built the pyramids, one feels that he must (to put it mildly) have been a clever man. We look at Blake's picture of the man, and with a start behold the face of an idiot. Nay, we behold even the face of an evil idiot, a leering, half-witted face with no chin and the protuberant nose of a pig. Blake declared that he drew this face from a real spirit, and I see no reason to doubt that he did. But if he did, it was not really the man who built the pyramids; it was not any spirit with whom a gentleman ought to wish to be on intimate terms. That vision of swinish silliness was really a bad vision to have, it left a smell of demoniac silliness behind it. I am very sure that it left Blake sillier than it found him.

In this way, rightly or wrongly, I explain the chaos and occasional weakness which perplexes Blake's critics and often perplexed Blake himself. I think he suffered from the great modern loneliness and scepticism which is the root of the sorrows of the mere spiritualist. The tragedy of the spiritualist simply is that he has to know his gods before he loves them. But a man ought to love his gods before he is sure that there are any. The sublime words of St John's Gospel permit of a sympathetic parody; if a man love not God whom he has not seen, how shall he love God whom he has seen? If we do not delight in Santa Claus even as a fancy, how can we expect to be happy even if we find that he is a fact? But a mystic like Blake simply puts up a placard for the whole universe, like an old woman letting lodgings. The mansion of his mind was indeed a magnificent one; but no one must be surprised if the first man that walked into it was "the man who built the pyramids," the man with the face of a moon-calf. And whether or no he built the pyramids, he unbuilt the house.

But this conclusion touching Blake's original sanity but incidental madness brings us abruptly in contact with the larger question of how far his soul and creed gained or suffered from his whole position; his heterodoxy, his orthodoxy, his attitude towards his age. Properly to do all this we must do now at the end of this book what ought (but the form of the book forbade) more strictly to have been done at the beginning; we must speak as shortly as possible about the actual age in which Blake lived. And we cannot do it without saying something, which we will say as briefly as possible, of that whole great western society and tradition to which he belonged and we belong equally; that Christendom or continent of Europe which is at once too big for us to measure and too close for us to understand.

What was the eighteenth century? Or rather (to speak less mechanically and with more intelligence), what was that mighty and unmistakable phase or mood through which western society was passing about the time that William Blake became its living child? What was that persistent trend or spirit which all through the eighteenth century lifted itself like a very slow and very smooth wave to the deafening breaker of the French Revolution? Of course it meant something slightly different to all its different children. Let us here ask ourselves what it meant to Blake, the poet, the painter, and the dreamer. Let us try to state the thing as nearly as possible in terms of his spirit and in relation to his unique work in this world.

Every man of us today is three men. There is in every modern European three powers so distinct as to be almost personal, the trinity of our earthly destiny. The three may be rudely summarised thus. First and nearest to us is the Christian, the man of the historic church, of the creed that must have coloured our minds incurably whether we regard it (as I do) as the crown and combination of the other two, or whether we regard it as an accidental superstition which has remained for two thousand years. First, then, comes the Christian; behind him comes the Roman, the citizen of that great cosmopolitan realm of reason and order in the level and equality of which Christianity arose. He is the stoic who is so much sterner than the anchorites. He is the republican who is so much prouder than kings. He it is that makes straight roads and clear laws, and for whom good sense is good enough. And the third man – he is harder to speak of. He has no name, and all true tales of him are blotted out; yet he walks behind us in every forest path and wakes within us when the wind wakes at night. He is the origins – he is the man in the forest. It is no part of our subject to elaborate the point; but it may be said in passing that the chief claim of Christianity is exactly this – that it revived the pre-Roman madness, yet brought into it the Roman order. The gods had really died long before Christ was born. What had taken their place was simply the god of government – Divus Caesar. The pagans of the real Roman Empire were nothing if not respectable. It is said that when Christ was born the cry went through the world that Pan was dead. The truth is that when Christ was born Pan for the first time began to stir in his grave. The pagan gods had become pure fables when Christianity gave them a new lease of life as devils. I venture to wager that if you found one man in such a society who seriously believed in the personal existence of Apollo, he was probably a Christian. Christianity called to a kind of clamorous resurrection all the old supernatural instincts of the forests and the hill. But it put upon this occult chaos the Roman idea of balance and sanity. Thus, marriage was a sacrament, but mere sex was not a sacrament as it was in many of the frenzies of the forest. Thus wine was a sacrament with Christ; but drunkenness was not a sacrament as with Dionysus. In short, Christianity (merely historically seen) can best be understood as an attempt to combine the reason of the market-place with the mysticism of the forest. it was an attempt to accept all the superstitions that are necessary to man and to be philosophic at the end of them. Pagan Rome has sought to bring order or reason among men. Christian Rome sought to bring order and reason among gods.

GIVEN these three principles, the epoch we discuss can be defined. The eighteenth century was primarily the return of reason – and of Rome. it was the coming to the top of the stoic and civic element in that triple mixture. It was full, like the Roman world, of a respect for law. Note that the priest still wears, in the main, the popular garb of the Middle Ages: but the lawyer still wears the head-dress of the eighteenth century. Yet while the Roman world was full of rule it was also full of revolution. But indeed the two things necessarily go together. The English used to boast that they had achieved a constitutional revolution; but every revolution must necessarily be a constitutional revolution, in so far that it must have reference to some antecedent theory of justice. A man must have rights before he can have wrongs. So it may be constantly remarked that the countries which have done most to spread legal generalisations and judicial decisions are those most filled with political fury and potential rebellion – Rome, for instance, and France. Rome planted in every tribe and village the root of the Roman law at the very time when her own town was torn with faction and bloody with partisan butcheries. France forced intellectually on nearly all Europe an excellent code of law, and she did it when her own streets were hardly cleared of corpses, when she was in a panting pause between two pulverizing civil wars. And, on the other hand, you may remark that the countries where there is no revolution are the countries where there is no law; where mental chaos has clouded every intelligible legal principle – such countries as Morocco and modern England.

The eighteenth century, then, ended in revolution because it began in law. It was the age of reason, and therefore the age of revolt. It is needless to say how systematically it revived all the marks and motives of that ancient pagan society in which Christianity first arose. Its greatest art was oratory, its favourite affectation was severity. Its pet virtue was public spirit, its pet sin political assassination. It endured the pompous, but hated the fantastic; it had pure contempt for anything that could be called obscure. To a virile mind of that epoch, such as Dr Johnson or Fox, a poem or picture that did not at once explain itself was simply like a gun that did not go off or a clock that stopped suddenly: it was simply a failure, fit for indifference or for a fleeting satire. In spite of their solid convictions (for which they died) the men of that time always used the word "enthusiast" as a term of scorn. All that we call mysticism they called madness. Such was the eighteenth-century civilisation; such was the strict and undecorated frame from which look at us the blazing eyes of William Blake.

So far Blake and his century are a mere contrast. But here we must remember that the three elements of Europe are not the strata of a rock, but the strands of a rope; since all three have existed not one of them has ever appeared entirely unmixed. You may call the pagan, but Renaissance

Michelangelo cannot be imagined as anything but a Christian. You may call Thomas Aquinas Christian, but you cannot say exactly what he would have been without Aristotle the pagan. You may, even in calling Virgil the poet of Roman dignity and good sense, still ask whether he did not remember something older than Rome when he spoke of the good luck of him who knew the field gods and the old man of the forest. In the same way there was even in the eighteenth century an element of the purely Christian and an element of the purely primitive. And, as it happens, both these non-rational (or non-Roman) strains in the eighteenth century are particularly important in considering the mental make-up of William Blake. For the first alien strain in this century practically represents all that is effective and fine in this great genius, the second strain represents without question all that is doubtful, all that is irritating, and all that is ineffective in him.

IN the eighteenth century there were two elements not taken from the Roman stoic or the Roman citizen. The first was what our century calls humanitarianism – what that century called "the tear of sensibility." The old pagan commonwealths were democratic, but they were not in the least humanitarian. They had no tears to spare for a man at the mercy of the community; they reserved all their anger and sympathy for the community at the mercy of a man. That individual compassion for an individual case was a pure product of Christianity; and when Voltaire flung himself with fury into the special case of Calas, he was drawing all his energies from the religion that he denied. A Roman would have rebelled for Rome, but not for Calas. This personal humanitarianism is the relic of Christianity – perhaps (if I may say so) the dregs of Christianity. Of this humanitarianism or sentimentalism, or whatever it can best be called, Blake was the enthusiastic inheritor. Being the great man that he was, he naturally anticipated lesser men than himself; and among the men less than himself I should count Shelley, for instance, and Tolstoy. He carried his instinct of personal kindness to the point of denouncing war as such –

> "Naught can deform the human race
> Like time Armourer's iron brace."

Or, again –

> "The strongest poison ever known
> Came from Caesar's iron crown."

No pagan republican, such as those on whom the eighteenth-century ethic was founded, could have made head or tail of this mere humanitarian horror. He could not even have comprehended this idea – that war is immoral when it is not unjust. You cannot find this sentiment in the pagans of antiquity, but you can find it in the pagans of the eighteenth century; you can find it in the speeches of Fox, the soliloquies of Rousseau and even in the sniggering of Gibbon. Here is an element of the eighteenth century which is derived darkly but indubitably from Christianity, and in which Blake strongly shares. Regulus has returned to be tortured and pagan Rome is saved; but Christianity thinks a little of Regulus. A man must be pitied even when he must be killed. That individual compassion provoked Blake to violent and splendid lines –

> "And the slaughtered soldier's cry
> Runs in blood down palace walls."

The eighteenth century did not find that pity where it found its pagan liberty and its pagan law. It took this out of the very churches that it violated and from the desperate faith that it denied. This irrational individual pity is the purely Christian element in the eighteenth century. This irrational individual pity is the purely Christian element in William Blake.

And second, there was another eighteenth-century element that was neither of Christian nor of pagan Rome. It was from the origins; it had been in the world through the whole history of paganism and Christianity; it had been in the world, but not of it. This element appeared popularly in the eighteenth century in an extravagant but unmistakable shape; the element can be summed up in one word – Cagliostro. No other name is quite so adequate; but if anyone desires a nobler name (a very noble one), we may say – Swedenborg. There was in the eighteenth century, despite its obvious good sense, this strain of a somewhat theatrical thaumaturgy. The history of that element is, in the most literal sense of the word, horribly interesting. For it all works back to the mere bogey feeling of the beginnings. It is amusing to remark that in the eighteenth century for the first time start up a number of societies which calmly announce that they have existed almost from the beginning of the world. Of these, of course, the best known instance is the Freemasons; according to their own account they began with the Pyramids; but according to everyone else's account that can be effectively collected, they began with the eighteenth century. Nevertheless the Freemasons are right in the spirit even if they are wrong in the letter. There is a tradition of things analogous to mystical masonry throughout all the historic generations of Paganism and Christianity. There is a definite tradition outside Christianity, not of rationalism, but of paganism, paganism in the original and frightful forest sense – pagan magic. Christianity, rightly or wrongly, always discouraged it on the ground that it was, or tended to be, black magic. That is not here our concern. The point is that this non-Christian supernaturalism, whether it was good or bad, was continuous in spite of Christianity. Its signs and traces can be seen in every age: it hung like a huge fume, in many monstrous forms, over the dying Roman Empire: it was the energy in the Gnostics who so nearly captured Christianity, and who were persecuted for their pessimism; in the full sunlight of the living Church it dared to carve its symbols upon the tombs of the Templars; and when the first sects raised their heads at the Reformation, its ancient and awful voice was heard.

Now the eighteenth century was primarily the release (as its leaders held) of reason and nature from the control of the Church. But when the Church was once really weakened, it was the release of many other things. It was not the release of reason only, but of a more ancient unreason. It was not the release of the natural, but also of the supernatural, and also, alas! of the unnatural. The heathen mystics hidden for two thousand years came out of their caverns – and Freemasonry was founded. It was entirely innocent in the manner of its foundation; but so were all the other resurrections of this ancestral occultism. I give but one obvious instance out of many. The idea of enslaving another human soul, without lifting a finger or making a gesture of force, of enslaving a soul simply by willing its slavery, is an idea which all healthy human societies would regard and did regard as hideous and detestable, if true. Throughout all the Christian ages the witches and warlocks claimed this abominable power and boasted of it. They were (somewhat excusably) killed for their boasting. The eighteenth-century rationalist movement came, intent, thank God, upon much cleaner things, upon common justice and right reason in the state. Nevertheless it did weaken Christianity, and in weakening Christianity it uplifted and protected the wizard. Mesmer stepped forward, and for the first time safely affirmed this infamous power to exist: for the first time a warlock could threaten spiritual tyranny and not be lynched. Nevertheless, if a mesmerist really had the powers which some mesmerists have claimed, and which most novels give to him, there is (I hope) no doubt at all that any decent mob would drown him like a witch.

The revolt of the eighteenth century, then, did not merely release naturalism, but a certain kind of supernaturalism also. And of this particular kind of supernaturalism, Blake is particularly the heir. Its coarse embodiment is Cagliostro. Its noble embodiment is Swedenborg. But in both cases it can be remarked that the mysticism marks an effort to escape from or even to forget the historic Christian, and especially the Catholic Church. Cagliostro, being a man of mean spirituality, separated himself from Catholicism by rearing against it a blazing pageant of mystical paganism, of triangles, secret seals, Eleusinian initiation, and all the vulgar refinements of a secret society.

Swedenborg, being a man of large and noble spirituality, marked his separation from Catholicism by inventing out of his own innocence and genius nearly all the old Catholic doctrines, sincerely believing them to be his own discoveries. It is startling to note how near Swedenborg was to Catholicism – in his insistence on free will, for instance, on the humanity of the incarnate God, and on the relative and mystical view of the Old Testament. There was in Blake a great deal of Swedenborg (as he would have been the first to admit), and there was, occasionally, a little of Cagliostro. Blake did not belong to a secret society: for, to tell the truth, he had some difficulty in belonging to any society. But Blake did talk a secret language. He had something of that haughty and oligarchic element in his mysticism which marked the old pagan secret societies and which marks the Theosophists and oriental initiates to this day. There was in him, besides the beneficent wealth of Swedenborg, some touch of Cagliostro and the Freemasons. These things Blake did inherit from that break up of belief that can be called the eighteenth century: we will debit him with these as an inheritance. And when we have said this we have said everything that can be said of any debt he owed. His debts are cleared here. His estate is cleared with this payment. All that follows is himself.

If a man has some fierce or unfamiliar point of view, he must, even when lie is talking about his cat, begin with the origin of the cosmos; for his cosmos is as private as his cat. Horace could tell his pupils to plunge into the middle of the thing, because he and they were agreed about the particular kind of thing; the author and his readers substantially sympathised about the beauty of Helen or the duties of Hector. But Blake really had to begin at the beginning, because it was a different beginning. This explains the extraordinary air of digression and irrelevancy which can be observed in some of the most direct and sincere minds. It explains the bewildering allusiveness of Dante; the galloping parentheses of Rabelais; the gigantic prefaces of Mr Bernard Shaw. The brilliant man seems more lumbering and elaborate than anyone else, because he has something to say about everything. The very quickness of his mind makes the slowness of his narrative. For he finds sermons in stones, in all the paving stones of the street he plods along. Every fact or phrase that occurs in the immediate question carries back his mind to the ages and the initial power. Because he is original he is always going back to the origins.

Take, for instance, Blake's verse rather than his pictorial art. When the average sensible person reads Blake's verse, he simply comes to the conclusion that he cannot understand it. But in truth he has a much better right to offer this objection to Blake than to most of the slightly elusive or eccentric writers to whom he also offers it. Blake is obscure in a much more positive and practical sense than Browning is obscure – or, in another manner, Mr Henry James is obscure. Browning is generally obscure through an almost brutal

1. Elohim creating Adam 1795. *Coloured monotype*, 1795

2. Illustration for 'American Prophecy',
'The Terror Answered'. *Relief etching with ink and watercolour wash*, 1793

3. Hecate. *Monotype, with watercolour*, 1795

4. The Ancient of Days.
Relief etching with ink and watercolour wash, 1793

5. The Third Temptation. *Watercolour illustration, (no date)*

6. Illustration for 'Jerusalem', 'Every Ornament of Perfection'.
Relief etching with watercolour and ink wash, 1804–20

eagerness to get to big truths, which leads him to smash a sentence and leave only bits of it. Mr Henry James is obscure because he wishes to trace tiny truths by a dissection for which human language (even in his exquisite hands) is hardly equal. In short, Browning wishes almost unscrupulously to get to the point. Mr James refuses to admit (on the mere authority of Euclid) that the point is indivisible. But Blake's obscurity is startlingly different to both, it is at once more simple and more impenetrable. It is not a different diction but a different language. It is not that we cannot understand the sentences; it is that we often misunderstand the words. The obscurity of Blake commonly consists in the fact that the actual words used mean one thing in Blake and quite another thing in the dictionary. Mr Henry James wants to split hairs; Browning wants to tear them up by the roots. But in Blake the enigma is at once plainer and more perplexing; it is simply this, that if Blake says "hairs" he may not mean hairs, but something else – perhaps peacocks' feathers. To quote but one example out of a thousand; when Blake uses the word" devils" he generally means some particularly exalted order of angels such as preside over energy and imagination.

Part II

A VERBAL accident has confused the mystical with the mysterious. Mysticism is generally felt vaguely to be itself vague – a thing of clouds and curtains, of darkness or concealing vapours, of bewildering conspiracies or impenetrable symbols. Some quacks have indeed dealt in such things: but no true mystic ever loved darkness rather than light. No pure mystic ever loved mere mystery. The mystic does not bring doubts or riddles: the doubts and riddles exist already. We all feel the riddle of the earth without anyone to point it out. The mystery of life is the plainest part of it. The clouds and curtains of darkness, the confounding vapours, these are the daily weather of this world. Whatever else we have grown accustomed to, we have grown accustomed to the unaccountable. Every stone or flower is a hieroglyphic of which we have lost the key; with every step of our lives we enter into the middle of some story which we are certain to misunderstand. The mystic is not the man who makes mysteries but the man who destroys them. The mystic is one who offers an explanation which may be true or false, but which is always comprehensible – by which I mean, not that it is always comprehended, but that it always can be comprehended, because there is always something to comprehend. The man whose meaning remains mysterious fails, I think, as a mystic: and Blake, as we shall see, did, for certain peculiar reasons of his own, often fail in this way. But even when he was himself hard to be understood, it was never through himself not understanding: it was never because he was vague or mystified or groping, that he was unintelligible. While his utterance was not only dim but dense, his opinion was not only clear, but even cocksure. You and I may be a little vague about the relations of Albion to Jerusalem, but Blake is as certain about them as Mr Chamberlain about the relations of Birmingham to the British Empire. And this can be said for his singular literary style even at his worst, that we always feel that he is saying something very plain and emphatic, even when we have not the wildest notion of what it is.

There is one element always to be remarked in the true mystic, however disputed his symbolism, and that is its brightness of colour and clearness of shape. I mean that we may be doubtful about the significance of a triangle or the precise lesson conveyed by a crimson cow. But in the work of a real mystic the triangle is a hard mathematical triangle not to be mistaken for a cone or a polygon. The cow is in colour a rich incurable crimson, and in shape unquestionably a cow, not to be mistaken for any of its evolutionary relatives, such as the buffalo or the bison. This can be seen very clearly, for instance, in the Christian art of illumination as practised at its best in the thirteenth and fourteenth centuries. The Christian decorators, being true mystics, were chiefly concerned to maintain the reality of objects. For the highest dogma of the spiritual is to affirm the material. By plain outline and positive colour those pious artists strove chiefly to assert that a cat was truly in the eyes of God a cat and that a dog was pre-eminently doggish. This decision of tint and outline belongs not only to Blake's pictures, but even to his poetry. Even in his descriptions there is no darkness, and practically, in the modern sense, no distance. All his animals are as absolute as the animals on a shield of heraldry. His lambs are of unsullied silver, his lions are of flaming gold. His lion may lie down with his lamb, but he will never really mix with him.

Really to make this point clear one would have to go back to the twelfth century, or perhaps to Plato. Metaphysics must be avoided; they are too exciting. But the root of the matter can be pretty well made plain by one word. The whole difference is between the old meaning and the new meaning of the word "Realist." In modern fiction and science a Realist means a man who begins at the outside of a thing: sometimes merely at the end of a thing, knowing the monkey only by its tail or the motor by its smell. In the twelfth century a Realist meant exactly the opposite; it meant a man who began at the inside of a thing. The mediaeval philosopher would only have been interested in a motor because it moved. He would have been interested (that is) only in the central and original idea of a motor – in its ultimate motorishness. He would have been concerned with a monkey only because of its monkeyhood; not because it was like man but because it was unlike. If he saw an elephant he would not say in the modern style, "I see before me a combination of the tusks of a wild boar in unnatural development, of the long nose of the tapir needlessly elongated, of the tail of the cow unusually insufficient," and so on. He would merely see an essence of elephant. He would believe that this light and fugitive elephant of an instant, as dancing and fleeting as the May-fly in May, was nevertheless the shadow of an eternal elephant, conceived and created by God. When you have quite realised this ancient sense in the reality of an elephant, go back and read William Blake's poems about animals, as, for instance, about the lamb and about the tiger. You will see quite clearly that he is talking of an eternal tiger, who rages and rejoices for ever in the sight of

God. You will see that he is talking of an eternal and supernatural lamb, who can only feed happily in the fields of Heaven.

It is exactly here that we find the full opposition to that modern tendency that can fairly be called "Impressionism." Impressionism is scepticism. It means believing one's immediate impressions at the expense of one's more permanent and positive generalisations. It puts what one notices above what one knows. It means the monstrous heresy that seeing is believing. A white cow at one particular instant of the evening light may be gold on one side and violet on the other. The whole point of Impressionism is to say that she really is a gold and violet cow. The whole point of Impressionism is to say that there is no white cow at all. What can we tell, it cries, beyond what we can see? But the essence of Mysticism is to insist that there is a white cow, however veiled with shadow or painted with sunset gold. Blessed are they who have seen the violet cow and who yet believe in the white one. To the mystic a white cow has a sort of solid whiteness, as if the cow were made out of frozen milk. To him a white horse has a solid whiteness as if he were cut out of the firm English chalk, like the White Horse in the valley of King Alfred. The cow's whiteness is more important than anything except her cowishness. If Blake had ever introduced a white cow into one of his pictures, there would at least have been no doubt about either of those two elements. Similarly there would have been no doubt about them in any old Christian illumination. On this point he is at one with all the mystics and with all the saints.

This explanation is really essential to the understanding of Blake, because to the modern mind it is so easy to understand him in the opposite sense. In the ordinary modern meaning Blake's symbols are not symbols at all. They are not allegories. An allegory nowadays means taking something that does not exist as a symbol of something that does exist. We believe, at least most of us do, that sin does exist. We believe (on highly insufficient grounds) that a dragon does not exist. So we make the unreal dragon an allegory of the real sin. But that is not what Blake meant when he made the lamb the symbol of innocence. He meant that there really is behind the universe an eternal image called the Lamb, of which all living lambs are merely the copies or the approximation. He held that eternal innocence to be an actual and even an awful thing. He would not have seen anything comic, any more than the Christian Evangelist saw anything comic, in talking about the Wrath of the Lamb. If there were a lamb in one of Æsop's fables, Æsop would never be so silly as to represent him as angry. But Christianity is more daring than Æsop, and the wrath of the Lamb is its great paradox. If there is an immortal lamb, a being whose simplicity and freshness are forever renewed, then it is truly and really a more creepy idea to horrify that being into hostility than to defy the flaming dragon or challenge darkness or the sea. No old wolf or world-worn lion is so awful as a creature that is always young – a creature that is always newly born. But the main point here is simpler. It is merely that Blake did not mean that meekness was true and the lamb only a pretty fable. If anything he meant that meekness was a mere shadow of the everlasting lamb. The distinction is essential to anyone at all concerned for this rooted spirituality which is the only enduring sanity of mankind. The personal is not a mere figure for the impersonal; rather the impersonal is a clumsy term for something more personal than common personality. God is not a symbol of goodness. Goodness is a symbol of God.

Some very odd passages in Blake become clear if we keep this in mind. I do not wish in this book to dwell unduly on the other side of Blake, the literary side. But there are queer facts worth remarking, and this is one of them. Blake was sincere; if he was insane he was insane with the very solidity and completeness of his sincerity. And the quaintest mark of his sincerity is this, that in his poetry he constantly writes things that look like mere mistakes. He writes one of his most colossal convictions and the average reader thinks it is a misprint. To give only one example not connected with the matter in hand, the fine though somewhat frantic poem called "The Everlasting Gospel" begins exactly as the modern humanitarian and essential Christian would like it to begin –

> "The vision of Christ that thou dost see
> Is my vision's greatest enemy."

It goes on (to the modern Christian's complete satisfaction) with denunciations of priests and praise of the pure Gospel Jesus; and then comes a couplet like this –

> "Thine is the friend of all mankind,
> Mine speaks in parables to the blind."

And the modern humanitarian Christian finds the orthodox Christ calmly rebuked because he is the friend of all mankind. The modern Christian simply blames the printer. He can only suppose that the words "Thine" and "Mine" have been put in each other's places by accident. Blake, however, as it happens, meant exactly what he said. His private vision of Christ was the vision of a violent and mysterious being, often indignant and occasionally disdainful.

> "He acts with honest disdainful pride,
> And that is the cause that Jesus died;
> Had he been Antichrist, creeping Jesus,
> He would have done anything to please us,
> Gone sneaking into their synagogues,

And not use the elders and priests like dogs."

When the reader has fully realised this idea of a fierce and mysterious Jesus, he may then see the sense in the statement that this Jesus speaks in parables to the blind while the lower and meaner Jesus pretends to be the friend of all men. But you have to know Blake's doctrine before you can understand two lines of his poetry.

Now in the point which is here prominently before us there is a quotation (indeed there is more than one) which follows this same fantastic line. Let the ordinary modern man, who is, generally speaking, not a materialist and not a mystic, read first these two lines from the poem falsely called "The Auguries of Innocence" –

"God appears and God is light
To those poor souls that dwell in night."

He will not find anything objectionable in that, at any rate; probably he will bow his head slightly to a truism, as if he were in church. Then he will read the next two lines –

"But does a human form display
To those that dwell in realms of day."

And there the modern man will sit down suddenly on the sofa and come finally to the conclusion that William Blake was mad and nothing else.

But those last two lines express all that is best in Blake and all that is best in all the tradition of the mystics. Those two lines explain perfectly all that I have just pointed out concerning the palpable visions and the ponderous cherubim. This is the point about Blake that must be understood if nothing else is understood. God for him was not more and more vague and diaphanous as one came near to Him. God was more and more solid as one came near. When one was far off one might fancy Him to be impersonal. When one came into personal relation one knew that He was a person. The personal God was the fact. The impersonal God of the Pantheists was a kind of condescending symbol. According to Blake (and there is more in the mental attitude than most modern people will willingly admit) this vague cosmic view is a mere merciful preparation for the old practical and personal view. God is merely light to the merely unenlightened. God is a man to the enlightened. We are permitted to remain for a time evolutionary or pantheist until the time comes when we are worthy to be anthropomorphic.

Understand this Blake conception that the Divine is most bodily and definite when we really know it, and the severe lines and sensational literalism of his other and more pictorial work will be easily understood. Naturally his divinities are definite, because he thought that the more they were definite, the more they were divine. Naturally God was not to him a hazy light breaking through the tangle of the evolutionary undergrowth, nor a blinding brilliancy in the highest place of the heavens. God was to him the magnificent old man depicted in his dark and extraordinary illustrations of "Job," the old man with the monstrous muscles, the mild stern eyebrows, the long smooth silver hair and beard. In the dialogues between Jehovah and Job there is little difference between the two ponderous and palpable old men, except that the vision of Deity is a little more solid than the human being. But then Blake held that Deity is more solid than humanity. He held that what we call the ideal is not only more beautiful but more actual than the real. The ordinary educated modern person staring at these "Job" designs can only say that God is a mere elderly twin brother of Job. Blake would have at once retorted that Job was an image of God.

ON consideration I incline to think that the best way to summarise the art of Blake from its most superficial to its most subtle phase would be simply to take one quick characteristic picture and discuss it fully; first its title and subject, then its look and shape, then its main principles and implications. Let us take as a good working example the weird picture which is reproduced on one of the pages of Gilchrist's "Life of Blake."

Now the obvious, prompt, and popular view of Blake is very well represented by the mere title of the picture. The first thing any ordinary person will notice about it is that it is called "The Ghost of a Flea"; and the ordinary person will be very justifiably amused. This is the first fact about William Blake – that he is a joke; and it is a fact by no means to be despised. Simply considered as a puzzle or parlour game, Blake is extraordinarily entertaining. I have known many cultivated families made happy on winter evenings by trying to understand the poem called "The Mental Traveller," or wondering what can be the significance of the stanza that runs:

> "Little Mary Bell had a fairy in a nut,
> Long John Brown had the devil in his gut;
> Long John Brown loved little Mary Bell,
> And the fairy drew the devil into the nutshell."

The first fact is that we are puzzled and also honestly amused. It is as if we had a highly eccentric neighbour in the next garden. Long before we like him we like gossiping about him. And the mere title, "The Ghost of a Flea," represents all that makes Blake a centre of literary gossip.

And now, having enjoyed the oddity of the title, let us look at the picture. Let us attempt to describe, so far as it can be done in words instead of lines, what Blake thought that the ghost of a flea would be like. The scene suggests a high and cheerless corridor, as in some silent castle of giants. Through this a figure, naked and gigantic, is walking with a high-shouldered and somewhat stealthy stride. In one hand the creature has a peculiar curved knife of a cruel shape; in the other he has a sort of stone basin. The most striking line in the composition is the hard long curve of the spine, which goes up without a single flicker to the back of the brutal head, as if the whole back view were built like a tower of stone. The face is in no sense human. It has something that is aquiline and also something that is swinish; its eyes are alive with a moony glitter that is entirely akin to madness. The thing seems to be passing a curtain and entering a room.

With this we may mark the second fact about Blake – that if his only object is to make our flesh creep, he does it well. His bogeys are good reliable bogeys. There is really something that appeals to the imagination about this notion of the ghost of a flea being a tall vampire stalking through tall corridors at night. We have found Blake an amusing madman and now an interesting madman; let us go on with the process.

The third thing to note about this picture is that for Blake time ghost of a flea means the idea or principle of a flea. The principle of a flea (so far as we can see it) is bloodthirstiness, the feeding on the life of another, the fury of the parasite. Fleas may have other nobler sentiments and meditations, but we know nothing about them. The vision of a flea is a vision of blood; and that is what Blake has made of it. This is the next point, then, to be remarked in his makeup as a mystic; he is interested in the ideas for which such things stand. For him the tiger means an awful elegance; for him the tree means a silent strength.

If it be granted that Blake was interested, not in the flea, but in the idea of the flea, we can proceed to the next step, which is a particularly important one. Every great mystic goes about with a magnifying glass. He sees every flea as a giant – perhaps rather as an ogre. I have spoken of the tall castle in which these giants dwell; but, indeed, that tall tower is the microscope. It will not be denied that Blake shows the best part of a mystic's attitude in seeing that the soul of a flea is ten thousand times larger than a flea. But the really interesting point is much more striking. It is the essential point upon which all primary understanding of the art of Blake really turns. The point is this: that the ghost of a flea is not only larger than a flea, the ghost of a flea is actually more solid than a flea. The flea himself is hazy and fantastic compared to the hard and massive actuality of his ghost. When we have understood this, we have understood the second of the great ideas in Blake – the idea of ideas.

To sum up Blake's philosophy in any phrase sufficiently simple and popular for our purpose is not at all easy. For Blake's philosophy was not simple. Those who imagine that because he was always talking about lambs and daisies, about Jesus and little children, that therefore he held a simple gospel of goodwill, entirely misunderstand the whole nature of his mind. No man had harder dogmas; no one insisted more that religion must have theology. The Everlasting Gospel was far from being a simple gospel. Blake had succeeded in inventing in the course of about ten years as tangled and interdependent a system of theology as the Catholic Church has accumulated in two thousand. Much of it, indeed, be inherited from ancient heretics who were much more doctrinal than the orthodoxy which they opposed. Notable among these were the Gnostics, and in some degree the mad Franciscans who followed Joachim de Flor. Very few modern people would know an Akamoth or an Æon if they saw him. Yet one would really have to be on rather intimate terms with these old mystical gods and demons before one could move quite easily in the Cosmos which was familiar to Blake.

Let us, however, attempt to find a short and popular statement of the position of Blake and all such mystics. The plainest way of putting it, I think, is this: this school especially denied the authority of Nature. Some went the extreme length of the mad Manichaeans, and declared the material universe evil in itself. Some, like Blake, and most of the poets considered it as a shadow or illusion, a sort of joke of the Almighty. But whatever else Nature was, Nature was not our mother. Blake applies to her the strange words used by Christ to Mary, and says to Mother-Earth in many poems: "What have I to do with thee?" It is common to connect Blake and Wordsworth because of their ballads about babies and sheep. They were utterly opposite. If Wordsworth was the Poet of Nature, Blake was specially the Poet of Anti Nature. Against Nature he set a certain entity which he called Imagination; but the word as commonly used conveys very little of what he meant by it. He did not mean something shadowy or fantastic, but rather something clear-cut, definite, and unalterable. By Imagination, that is, he meant images; the eternal images of things. You might shoot all the lions on the earth; but you could not destroy the Lion of Judah, the Lion of the Imagination. You might kill all the lambs of the world and eat them; but you could not kill the Lamb of the Imagination, which was the Lamb of God, that taketh away the sins of the world. Blake's philosophy, in brief, was primarily the assertion that the ideal is more actual than the real: just as in Euclid the good triangle in the mind is a more actual (and more practical) than the bad triangle on the blackboard.

Many of Blake's pictures become intelligible (or as intelligible as they can become) if we keep this principle in mind. For instance, there is a fine design representing a naked and heroic youth of great beauty tracing something on the sand. The reader, when he looks at the title of it, is interested to discover that this is a portrait of Sir Isaac Newton. It was not so much of an affectation as it seems. Blake from his own point of view really did think that the Eternal Isaac Newton as God beheld him was more of an actuality than the terrestrial gentleman who happened to be elderly or happened by some sublunary accident to wear clothes. Therefore, when he calls it a "portrait" he is not, from his own point of view, talking nonsense. It is the form and feature of someone who exists and who is different from everyone else, just as if it were the ordinary oil-painting of an alderman.

The most important conception can be found in one sentence which he let fall as if by accident, "Nature has no outline, but imagination has." If a clear black line when looked at through a microscope was seen to be a ragged and confused edge like a mop or a doormat, then Blake would say, "So much the worse for the microscope." If pure lines existed only on the human mind, then Blake would say, "So much the better for the human mind." If the real earth grew damp and dubious when it met and mixed itself with the sea, so much the worse for the real earth. If the idea of clean-cut truth existed only in the intellect, that was the most actual place in which anything could exist. In short, Blake really insisted that man as the image of God had a right to impose form upon nature. He would have laughed to scorn the notion of the modern evolutionist – that Nature is to be permitted to impose formlessness upon man. For him the lines in a landscape were boundaries which he drew like frontiers, by his authority as the plenipotentiary ambassador of heaven. When he drew his line round Leviathan he was drawing the divine net around him; he tamed his bulls and lions even by creating them. And when he made in some picture a line between sea and land that does not exist in Nature, he was saying by supernatural right, "Thus far shalt thou come, and no farther, and here shall thy proud waves be stayed."

I SELECT the symbol of the sea partly because Blake was himself fond of such elemental images, and partly because it is an image especially appropriate to Blake's great conception of the outline in the eternal imagination. Nearly all phrases about the sea are specially and spiritually false. People talk of the sea as vast and vague, drifting and indefinite; as if the magic of it lay in having no lines or boundaries. But the spell of the sea upon the eye and the soul is exactly this: that it is the one straight line in nature. They talk of the infinite sea. Artistically it would be far truer to talk of an infinite haystalk; for the haystalk does slightly fade into a kind of fringe against the sky. But the horizon line is not only hard but *tight*, like a fiddle string. I have always a nervous fear that the sea-line will snap suddenly. And it is exactly this mathematical decision in the sea that makes it so romantic a background for fighting and human figures. England was called in Catholic days the garden of Mary. The garden is all the more beautiful because it is enclosed in four hard angular walls of sapphire or emerald. Any mere tuft or twig can curve with a curve that is incalculable. Any scrap of moss can contain in itself an irregularity that is infinite. The sea is the one thing that is really exciting because the sea is the one thing that is flat.

Whether, however, these conclusions can be accepted by the reader as true, they can at least be accepted as typifying the kind of thing which William Blake believed to be true. He would have felt the sea not as a waste but as a wall. Nature had no outline, but imagination had. And it was imagination that was trustworthy.

This definition explains other things. Blake was enthusiastically in favour of the French Revolution; yet he enthusiastically hated that school of sceptics which, in the opinion of many, made the Revolution possible. He did not mind Marat; but he detested Voltaire. The reason is obvious in the light of his views on Nature and Imagination. The Republican Idealists he liked because they were Idealists, because their abstract doctrines about justice and human equality were abstract doctrines. But the school of Voltaire was naturalistic; it loved to remind man of his earthly origin and even of his earthly degradation. The war, which Blake loved, was a war of the invisible against the visible. Valmy and Arcola were part of such a war; it was a war between the visible kings and the invisible Republic. But Voltaire's war was exactly the opposite; it was a discrediting of the invisible Church by the indecent exhibition of the real Church, with its fat friars or its foolish old women. Blake had no sympathy with this mere flinging of facts at a great conception. In a really powerful and exact metaphor he describes the powerlessness of this earthly and fragmentary sceptical attack.

> Mock on, mock on, Voltaire, Rousseau,
> Mock on, mock on, 'tis all in vain,
> You throw the sand against the wind
> And the wind blows it back again.

An excellent image for a mere attack by masses of detail.

There were some of Blake's intellectual conceptions which I have not professed either to admire or to defend. Some of his views were really what the old mediaeval world called heresies and what the modern world (with an equally healthy instinct but with less scientific clarity) calls fads. In either case the definition of the fad or heresy is not so very difficult. A fad or heresy is the exaltation of something which, even if true, is secondary or temporary in its nature against those things which are essential and eternal, those things which always prove themselves true in the long run. In short, it is the setting up of the mood against the mind. For instance: it is a mood, a beautiful and lawful mood, to wonder how oysters really feel. But it is a fad, an ugly and unlawful fad, to starve human beings because you will not let them eat oysters. It is a beautiful mood to feel impelled to assassinate Mr Carnegie; but it is a fad to maintain seriously that any private person has a right to do it. We all have emotional moments in which we should like to be indecent in a drawing-room; but it is faddist to turn all drawing-rooms into places in which one is indecent. We all have at times an almost holy temptation suddenly to scream out very loud; but it is heretical and pedantic really to go on screaming for the remainder of your natural life. If you throw one bomb you are only a murderer; but if you keep on persistently throwing bombs you are in awful danger of at last becoming a prig. It has been this trouble that has partly poisoned the people from which William Blake inherited, if not his blood, at least his civilization. The real trouble with Puritanism was not that it was a senseless prejudice nor yet altogether (as would seem superficially obvious) that it was a mere form of devil-worship. It was none of these things in its first and freshest motive.

Puritanism was an honourable mood; it was a noble fad. In other words, it was a highly creditable mistake. We have all felt the frame of mind in which one wishes to smash golden croziers and mitres merely because they are golden. We all know how natural it is at certain moments to feel a profound thirst to kick clergymen simply because they are clergymen. But if we seriously ask ourselves whether in the long run humanity is not happier with gold in its religion rather than mere drab, then we come to the conclusion that the gold on cross or cope does give more pleasure to most men than it gives pain, for a moment, to us. If we really ask ourselves if religions do not work better with a definite priesthood to do the drudgery of religion, we come to the conclusion that they do work better. Anti-clericalism is a generous and ideal mood; clericalism is a permanent and practical necessity. To put the matter in an easier and more everyday metaphor, it is natural for any poor Londoner to feel at times an abstract aspiration to beat the Lord Mayor of London. But it does not follow that it would really have been a kindness to poor Londoners to abolish the Lord Mayor's Show.

Now it is in this sense that we may truly say that Blake (upon one side of his mind) was something worse than a maniac – he was a faddist. He did permit aspirations or prejudices which are accidental or one-sided to capture and control him at the expense of things really more human and enduring: things which he shared with all the children of men. I do not allude to his supernaturalism; for on that he is in no sense alone, nor even specially eccentric. I do not refer to his love of the gorgeous, the terrible or even the secretive of temples, initiations, and hieroglyphic religion. For that sort of mystery is really quite popular and even democratic. That sort of secrecy is a very open secret.

It is usual to hear a man say in modern England that he has too much common sense to believe in ghosts. But common sense is in favour of a belief in ghosts, the common sense of mankind. It is usual to hear a man say that he likes common sense and does not like the mummeries and flummeries of church ritual. But common sense is in favour of mummery and ritualism, the common sense of mankind. The man who attempts to do without symbols is a prophet so austere and isolated as to be dangerously near to a madman. The man who does not believe in ghosts is a solitary fanatic and lonely dreamer among the sons of men. Therefore I do not in any sense count even his craziest visions or wildest symbols among the real fads or eccentricities of Blake. But he had mental attitudes which were really fads and eccentricities, in this essential sense, that they were not exaggerations of a general human feeling but definite denials of it. He did not lead humanity, but attacked or even obstructed it. Many instances might be given of the kind of thing I mean; there was something of it in Blake's persistent and even pedantic insistence that war as war is evil. There was something of Tolstoy in Blake; and that means something that is inhuman as well as something that is heroic. But his allusions to this were occasional and perhaps even accidental, and better cases could certainly be found. The essential of all the cases is, however, that when he went wrong it was as an intellectual and not as a poet.

Take, for example, his notion of going naked. Here I think Blake is merely a sort of hard theorist. Here, in spite of his imagination and his laughter, there was even a touch of the prig about him. He was obscene on principle. So to a great extent was Walt Whitman. A dictionary is supposed to contain all words, so it has to contain coarse words. "Leaves of Grass" was planned to praise all things, so it had to praise gross things. There was something of this pedantic perfection in Blake's escapades. As the hygienist insists on wearing Jäger clothes, he insisted on wearing no clothes. As the aesthete must wear sandals, he must wear nothing. He is not really lawless at all; he is bowing to the law of his own outlawed logic.

There is nothing at all poetical in this revolt. William Blake was a great and real poet; but in this point he was simply unpoetical. Walt Whitman was a great and real poet; but on this point he was prosaic and priggish. Two extraordinary men are not poets because they tear away the veil from sex. On the contrary it is because all men are poets that they all hang a veil over sex. The ploughman does not plough by night, because he does not feel specially romantic about ploughing. He does love by night, because he does feel specially romantic about sex. In this matter Blake was not only unpoetical, but far less poetical than the mass of ordinary men. Decorum is not an over-civilised convention. Decorum is not tame, decorum is wild, as wild as the wind at night.

> "Mysterious as the moons that rise
> At midnight in the pines of Var."

Modesty is too fierce and elemental a thing for the modern pedants to understand; I had almost said too savage a thing. It has in it the joy of escape and the ancient shyness of freedom. In this matter Blake and Whitman are merely among the modern pedants. In not admiring sexual reticence these two great poets simply did not understand one of the greatest poems of humanity.

I have given as an instance his disregard of the idea of mystery and modesty as involved in dress; it was an unpoetical thought that there should be no curtains of gold or scarlet round the shrine of the Holy Spirit. But there is stronger instances in his theology and philosophy. Thus he imbibed the idea common among early Gnostics and not unknown to Christian Science speculators of our day, that it was a confession of weakness in Christ to be crucified at all. If he had really attained divine life (so ran the argument) he ought to have attained immortal life; he ought to have lived for ever upon the earth. With an excess of what can only be called impudence, he even turned Gethsemane into a sort of moral breakdown; the sudden weakness which accepted death. The general claim that vices are poetical is largely unfounded; and this is an excellent example of how unpoetical is the vice of profanity. Blasphemy is not wild; blasphemy is in its nature prosaic. It consists in regarding in a commonplace manner something which other and happier people regard in a rapturous and imaginative manner. This is well exemplified in poor Blake and his Gnostic heresy about Jesus. In holding that Christ was weakened by being crucified he is certainly a pedant, and certainly not a poet. If there is one point on which the spirit of the poets and the poetic soul in all peoples is on the side of Christianity, it is exactly this one point on which Blake is against Christianity – "was crucified, dead and buried." The spectacle of a God dying is much more grandiose than the spectacle of a man living for ever. The former suggests that awful changes have really entered the alchemy of the universe; the latter is only vaguely reminiscent of hygienic octogenarians and Eno's Fruit Salts. Moreover, to the poet as to the child, death must be dreadful even if it is desirable. To talk (as some modern theosophists do) about death being nothing, the mere walking into another room, to talk like this is not only prosaic and profoundly un-Christian; it is decidedly vulgar. It is against the whole trend of the secret emotions of humanity. It is indecent, like persuading a decent peasant to go without clothes. There is more of the song and music of mankind in a clerk putting on his Sunday clothes than in a fanatic running naked down Cheapside. And there is more real mysticism in nailing down a coffin lid than in pretending, in mere rhetoric, to throw open the doors of death.

I have given two cases of the presence in Blake of these anti-human creeds which I call fads – the case of clothes and the case of the crucifixion. I could give a much larger number of them, but I think their nature is here sufficiently indicated. They are all cases in which Blake ceased to be a poet, through becoming entirely, instead of only partially, separated from the people. And this, I think, is certainly connected with that quality in him to which I referred in analysing the eighteenth century; I mean the element of oligarchy and fastidiousness in the mystics and masonries of that epoch. They were all founded in an atmosphere of degrees and initiations. The chief difference between Christianity and the thousand transcendental schools of today is substantially the same as the difference nearly two thousand years ago between Christianity and the thousand sacred rites and secret societies of the Pagan Empire. The deepest difference is this: that all the heathen mysteries are so far aristocratic, that they are understood by some, and not understood by others. The Christian mysteries are so far democratic that nobody understands them at all.

When we have fairly stated this doubtful and even false element in Blake's philosophy, we can go on with greater ease and thoroughness to state where the solid and genuine value of that philosophy lay. It consisted in its placid and positive defiance of materialism, a work upon which all the mystics, Pagan and Christian, have been employed from the beginning. It is not unnatural that they should have fallen into many errors, employed dangerous fallacies, and even ruined the earth for the sake of the cloudland. But the war in which they were engaged has been none the less the noblest and most important effort of human history, and in their whole army there was no greater warrior than Blake.

One of the strange and rooted contradictions of the eighteenth century is a combination between profound revolution and superficial conventionality. It might almost be said that the men of that time had altered morals long before they thought of altering manners. The French Revolution was especially French in this respect, that it was above all things a respectable revolution. Violence was excused; madness was excused; but eccentricity was inexcusable. These men had taken a king's head off his shoulders long before they had thought of taking the powder off their own heads. Danton could understand the Massacres of September, but he could not understand the worship of the Goddess of Reason or all the antics of the German madman Clootz. Robespierre grew tired of the Terror, but he never grew tired of shaving every morning. It is impossible to avoid the impression that this is rather a characteristic of the revolutions which really make a difference and defy the world. The same is true of that fallacious but most powerful and genuine English monument which was covered by the words Darwin and Evolution. If there was one striking thing about the fine old English agnostics, it was that they were entirely indifferent to alterations in the externals of pose or fashion, that they seem to have supposed that the huge intellectual overturn of agnosticism would leave the obvious respectability of life exactly as it was. They thought that one might entirely alter a man's head without in the least altering his hat. They thought that one might shatter the twin wings of an archangel without throwing the least doubt upon the twin whiskers of a mid-Victorian professor. And though there was undoubtedly a certain solemn humour about such a position, yet, on the whole, I think the mid-Victorian agnostics were employing the right kind of revolution. It is broadly a characteristic of all valuable new-fashioned opinions that they are brought in by old-fashioned men. For the sincerity of such men is proved by both facts – the fact that they do care about their new truth and the fact that they do not care about their old clothes. Herbert Spencer's philosophy is all the more serious because his appearance (to judge by his photographs) was quite startlingly absurd. And while the Tory caricatures were deriding Gladstone because he introduced very new-fangled legislation, they were also deriding him because he wore very antiquated collars.

But though this strange combination of convention in small things with revolt in big ones is not uncommon in hearty and human reformers, there is a quite special emphasis on this combination in the case of the eighteenth century. The very men who did deeds which were more dreadful and daring than we can dream to achieve, were the very men who spoke and wrote with a mincing propriety and almost effeminate fastidious distinction such as we should scarcely condescend to employ. The eighteenth-century man called the eighteenth-century woman "an elegant female"; but he was quite capable of saving her from a mad bull. He described his ideal republic as a place containing all the refined sensibilities of virtue with all the voluptuous seductions of pleasure. But he would be hacked with an axe and blown out of a gun to get it. He could pursue new notions with a certain solid and virile constancy, as if they were old ones. And the explanation is partly this: that however revolutionary, they were old ones – in this sense at least, that they involved the pursuit of some primary human hope to its original home. They powdered their hair because they really thought that a civilized man should be civilized – or, if you will, artificial. They spoke of "an elegant female" because they really thought, with their whole souls, that a female ought to be elegant. The old rebels preserved the old fashions – and among others the old fashion of rebelling. The new rebels, the revolutionists of our time, are intent upon introducing new fashions in boots, beds, food or furniture; so they have no time to rebel. But if we have once grasped this eighteenth-century element of the insistence upon the elegant female because she is elegant, we have got hold of a fundamental fact in the relation of that century to Blake.

It is instinctive to describe Blake as a fantastic artist; and yet there is a very real sense in which Blake is conventional. If any reader thinks the phrase paradoxical, he can easily discover that it is true; he can discover it simply by comparing Blake even in his most wild and arbitrary work with any merely modern artist who has the name of being wild; with Aubrey Beardsley or even with Rossetti. All Blake's heroes are conventional heroes made unconventionally heroic. All Blake's heroines are elegant females without their clothes. But in both cases they exaggerate and insist upon the traditional ideal of the sexes – the broad shoulders of the god and the broad hips of the goddess. Blake detested the sensuality of Rubens. But if he had been obliged to choose between the women of Rubens and the women of Rossetti, he would have flung himself on the neck of Rubens. For we have a false conception of what constitutes exaggeration. The end of the eighteenth century (being a dogmatic period) believed in certain things and exaggerated them. The end of the nineteenth century simply did not know what things to exaggerate; so it fell back upon merely underrating them. Blake tried to make Wallace look even bolder and fiercer than Wallace can possibly have looked. That was his exaggeration of Wallace. But Burne-Jones' exaggeration of Perseus is not an exaggeration at all. It is an under-statement; for the whole fascination of Burne-Jones' Perseus is that he looks frightened. Blake's figure of a woman is aggressively and monstrously womanly. That is its fascination, if it has any. But the fascination of a Beardsley woman (if she has any) is exactly that she is not quite a woman. So much of what we have meant by exaggeration is really diminution; so much of what we have meant by fancy is simply falling short of fact. The Burne-Jones' man is interesting because he is not quite brave enough to be a man. The Beardsley woman is interesting because she is not quite pretty enough to be a woman. But Blake's men are brave beyond all decency: and Blake's women are so swaggeringly bent on being beautiful that they become quite ugly in the process. If anyone wishes to know exactly what I mean, I recommend him to look at one of those extraordinary designs of nymphs in which a woman (or, as Blake loved to call it, the Female Form) is made to perform an impossible feat of acrobatics. It is impossible, but it is quite female; perhaps the words are not wholly inconsistent. A living serpent might perform such a piece of athletics; but even then only a female living serpent. But nobody would ask a Burne-Jones or Beardsley female to perform any athletics at all.

Blake in pictorial art was not a mere master of the moonstruck or the grotesque. On the contrary, he was, as artists go, exceptionally a champion of the smooth and sensible. In so far as being "modern" means being against the great conventions of mankind, indifferent to the difference of the sexes, or inclined to despise doctrinal outline, then there was never any man who was so little of a modern as Blake. He may have been mad; but there are varieties even in madness. There are madmen, like Blake, who go mad on health, and there are madmen who go mad on sickness.

The distinction is a solid one. You may think the queerly and partially clothed women of Aubrey Beardsley ugly. You may think the naked women of William Blake ugly. But you must perceive this peculiar and extraordinary effect about the women of William Blake, that they are women. They are exaggerated in the direction of the female form; they swing upon big hips; they let out and loosen long and luxuriant hair. Now the queer females of Aubrey Beardsley are queerest of all in this, that they are not even female. They are narrow where women have a curve and cropped where women have a head of hair. Blake's women are often anatomically impossible. But they are so far women that they could not possibly be anything else.

This comparison between Blake's art and such art as Aubrey Beardsley's is not an invidious impertinence, it is really an important distinction. Blake's work may be fantastic; but it is a fantasia on an old and recognisable air. It exaggerates characteristics. Blake's women are too womanish, his young men are too athletic, his old men are too preposterously old. But Aubrey Beardsley does not really exaggerate; he understates. His young men have less than the energy of youth. His women fascinate by the weakness of sex rather than by its strength. In short, if one is really to exaggerate the truth, one must have some truth to exaggerate. The decadent mystic produces an effect not by exaggerating but by distorting. True exaggeration is a thing both subtle and austere. Caricature is a serious thing; it is almost blasphemously serious. Caricature really means making a pig more like a pig than even God has made him. But anyone can make him not like a pig at all; anyone can create a weird impression by giving him the beard of a goat. In Aubrey Beardsley the artistic thrill (and there is an artistic thrill) consists in the fact that the women are not quite women nor the men quite men. Blake had absolutely no trace of this morbidity of deficiency. He never asks us to consider a tree magical because it is a stunted tree; or a man a magician merely because he has one eye. His form of fantasy would rather be to give a tree more branches than it could carry and to give a man bigger eyes than he could keep in his head. There is really a great deal of difference between the fantastic and the exaggerative. One may be fantastic by merely leaving something out. One might call it a fantasy if the official portrait of Wellington represented him without a nose. But one could hardly call it an exaggeration.

There is an everlasting battle in which Blake is on the side of the angels, and what is much more difficult and dangerous, on the side of all the sensible men. The question is so enormous and so important, that it is difficult to state even by reason of its reality. For in this world of ours we do not so much go on and discover small things; rather we go on and discover big things. It is the details that we see first; it is the design that we only see very slowly; and some men die never having seen it at all. We all wake up on a battle-field. We see certain squadrons in certain uniforms gallop past; we take an arbitrary fancy to this or that colour, to this or that plume. But it often takes us a long time to realise what the fight is about or even who is fighting whom. One may say, to keep up the metaphor, that many a man has joined the French army from love of the Horse Guards Blue; many an old fashioned eighteenth-century sailor has gone over to the Chinese merely because they wore pigtails. It is so easy to turn against what is really yourself for the sake of some accidental resemblance to yourself. You may envy the curled hair of Hercules; but do not envy curly hair until you wish that you were a nigger. You may regret that you have a short nose; but do not dream of its growing longer and longer till it is like the trunk of an elephant. Wait until you know what the battle is broadly about before you rush roaring after any advancing regiment. For a battle is a complicated thing; each army contains coats of different colour; each section of each army advances at a different angle. You may fancy that the Greens are charging the Blues exactly at the moment when both are combining to effect a fine military manoeuvre. You may conceive that two similar-looking columns are supporting each other at the very instant when they are about to blaze at each other with cannon, rifle, and revolver. So in the modern intellectual world we can see flags of many colours, deeds of manifold interest; the one thing we cannot see is the map. We cannot see the simplified statement which tells us what is the origin of all the trouble. How shall we manage to state in an obvious and alphabetical manner the ultimate query, the primordial pivot on which the whole modern problem turns? It cannot be done in long rationalistic words; they convey by their very sound the suggestion of something subtle. One must try to think of something in the way of a plain street metaphor or an obvious analogy. For the thing is not too hard for human speech; it is actually too obvious for human speech.

The fundamental fight in which, despite all this heat and headlong misunderstanding, William Blake is on the right side, is one which would require a book about the battle and not about William Blake. By an accident at once convenient and deceptive, it can largely be described as geographical as well as philosophical. It is crudely true that there are two types of mysticism, that of Christendom and that of Orientalism. Now this scheme of east and west is inadequate; but it does happen to fit in with the working facts. For the odd thing is this, not only are most of the merely modern movements of idealism Oriental, but their Orientalism is all that they have in common. They all come together, and yet their only apparent point of union is that they all come from the East. Thus a modern vegetarian is generally also a teetotaller, yet there is certainly no obvious intellectual connection between consuming vegetables and not consuming fermented vegetables. A drunkard, when lifted laboriously out of the gutter, might well be heard huskily to plead that he had fallen there through excessive devotion to a vegetable diet. On the other hand, a man might well be a practised and polished cannibal and still be a strict teetotaller. A subtle parallelism might doubtless be found; but the only quite obvious parallelism is that vegetarianism is Buddhist and teetotalism is Mahometan. In the same way, it is the cold truth that there is no kind of logical connection between being an Agnostic and being a Socialist. But it is the fact that the Chinese are as agnostic as oxen; and it is the fact that the Japanese are as socialistic as rats. These appalling ideas, that a man has no divine individual destiny, that making a minute item in the tribe or hive, is his only earthly destiny, these ideas do come all together out of the same quarter; they do in practise blow upon us out of the East, as cold and inhuman as the east wind.

Nevertheless, I do not accept this dull definition by locality; I think it is a spirit in Asia, and even a spirit that can be named. it is approximately described as an insane simplicity. In all these cases we find people attempting to perfect a thing solely by simplification; by obliterating special features : this cosmos is full of wingless birds, of hornless cattle, of hairless women, and colourless wine, all fading into a formless background. There is a Christian simplicity, of course, opposed to this pessimist simplicity. Both the western and eastern mystic may be called children; but the eastern child treads the sandcastle back into sand, and enjoys seeing the silver snowman melt back into muddy water. This return to chaos and a comfortless simplicity is the only intelligent meaning of the words reaction and reactionary. In this sense much of modern science is reaction, and most modern scientists are reactionaries. But where this reversion to the void can be seen most clearly is in all the semi-oriental sects to which I have referred. Teetotalism is a simplification; its objection to beer is not really that beer makes a man like a beast. On the contrary, its real objection is that beer most unmistakably separates a man from a beast. Vegetarianism is a simplification; the herb-eating Hindu saint does not really dislike the carnivorous habit because it destroys an animal. Rather, he dislikes it because it creates an animal; renews the special aims and appetites of the separate animal, man. Agnosticism, the ancient creed of Confucius, is a simplification; it is a shutting out of all the shadowy splendours and terrors; an Arcadian exclusiveness; *il faut cultiver son jardin.* Japanese patriotism, the blind collectivism of the tribe, is a simplification; it is an attempt to turn our turbulent and varied humanity into one enormous animal, with twenty million legs, but only one head. There is an utterly opposite kind of simplicity that springs from joy; but this kind of simplicity certainly is rooted in despair.

Now, for practical purposes, there is an antagonistic order of mysticism; that which celebrates personality, positive variety, and special emphasis: just as in broad fact the mystery of dissolution is emphasized and typified in the East, so in practice the mystery of concentration and identity is manifest in the historic churches of Christendom. Even the foes of Christianity would readily agree that Christianity is "personal" in the sense that a vulgar joke is "personal": that is corporeal, vivid, perhaps ugly. This being so, it has been broadly true that any mystic who broke with the Christian tradition tended to drift towards the eastern and pessimist tradition. In the Albigensian and other heresies the East crawled in with its serpentine combination of glitter and abasement, of pessimism and pleasure. Every dreamer who strayed outside the Christian order strayed towards the Hindu order, and every such dreamer found his dream turning to a nightmare. If a man wandered far from Christ he was drawn into the orbit of Buddha, the other great magnet of mankind – the negative magnet. The thing is true down to the latest and the most lovable visionaries of our own time; if they do not climb up into Christendom, they slide down into Tibet. The greatest poet now writing in the English language (and it is surely unnecessary to say that I mean Mr Yeats) has written a whole play round the statement, "Where there is nothing there is God." In this he sharply and purposely cuts himself off from the real Christian position, that where there is anything there is God.

But though, by an almost political accident, Oriental pessimism has been the practical alternative to the Christian type of transcendentalism, there is, and always has been, a third thing that was neither Christian in an orthodox sense nor Buddhistic in any sense. Before Christianity existed there was a European school of optimist mystics; among whom the great name is Plato. And ever since there have been movements and appearances in Europe of this healthier heathen mysticism, which did not shrink from the shapes of things or the emphatic colours of existence. Something of the sort was in the Nature worship of Renaissance philosophers; something of the sort may even have been behind the strange mixture of ecstacy and animality in the isolated episode of Luther. This solid and joyful occultism appears at its best in Swedenborg; but perhaps at its boldest and most brilliant in William Blake.

The present writer will not, in so important a matter, pretend to the absurd thing called impartiality; he is personally quite convinced that if every human being lived a thousand years, every human being would end up either in utter pessimistic scepticism or in the Catholic creed. William Blake, in his rationalist and highly Protestant age, was frequently reproached for his tenderness towards Catholicism; but it would have surprised him very much to be told that he would join it. But he would have joined it – if he had lived a thousand years, or even perhaps a hundred. He was on the side of historic Christianity on the fundamental question on which it confronts the East; the idea that personality is the glory of the universe and not its shame; that creation is higher than evolution, because it is more personal; that pardon is higher than Nemesis, because it is more personal; that the forgiveness of sins is essential to the communion of saints; and the resurrection of the body to the life everlasting. It was a mark of the old eastern initiations, it is still a mark of the grades and planes of our theosophical thinkers, that as a man climbs higher and higher, God becomes to him more and more formless, ethereal, and even thin. And in many of these temples, both ancient and modern, the final reward of serving the god through vigils and purifications, is that one is at last worthy to be told that the god doesn't exist.

Against all this emasculate mysticism Blake like a Titan rears his colossal figure and his earthquake voice. Through all the cloud and chaos of his stubborn symbolism and his perverse theories, through the tempest of exaggeration and the full midnight of madness, he reiterates with passionate precision that only that which is lovable can be adorable, that deity is either a person or a puff of wind, that the more we know of higher things the more palpable and incarnate we shall find them; that the form filling the heavens is the likeness of the appearance of a man. Much of what Blake thus wildly thundered has been put quietly and quaintly by Coventry Patmore, especially in that delicate and daring passage in which he speaks of the bonds, the simpleness and even the narrowness of God. The wise man will follow a star, low and large and fierce in the heavens; but the nearer he comes to it the smaller and smaller it will grow, till he finds it the humble lantern over some little inn or stable. Not till we know the high things shall we know how lowly they are. Meanwhile, the modern superior transcendentalist will find the facts of eternity incredible because they are so solid; he will not recognise heaven because it is so like the earth.

G K Chesterton

Autobiography

In *Autobiography* Chesterton describes his happy childhood, the intellectual 'doubts and morbidities' of his youth and his search for a true vocation.

He includes many anecdotes about his literary friends, Henry James, George Bernard Shaw and H G Wells.

But it is his quest for religious conviction and his conversion to Catholicism that is central to his story which he tells with great modesty, gentleness and intelligence.

Chaucer

Chesterton expounds the 'genius of Geoffrey Chaucer' in this literary biography that explores both the writer and his time. He claims that Chaucer and his Age were 'more sane, more normal and more cheerful than writers that came after him' and the characters he portrayed have an immediate contemporary relevance.

Beautifully and sensitively written, this biography about the 'Father of English Poetry' will inform and inspire.

G K Chesterton

Criticisms and Appreciations of the Works of Charles Dickens

Written with intelligence and authority, these twenty-three essays provide an insight into the works of the literary genius of Charles Dickens.

Chesterton greatly admired Dickens as a social prophet and defender of the common man. Here, he focuses both on the style and the ideology of Dickens and provides the critical insight into his work with his characteristic perceptive generosity. Chesterton is still regarded by many as one of the most accomplished and perceptive critics of Dickens.

As much about Chesterton's strongly held beliefs as about Dickens, this volume is sure to inform and give pleasure to advocates of both writers.

George Bernard Shaw

The book traces in some detail Shaw's work as a critic (puritanical opposition to Shakespeare) and as a dramatist.

Chesterton was ideally placed to write this critical biography of the literary works and political views of George Bernard Shaw. He was a personal friend and yet an ardent opponent of Shaw's progressive socialism. The lightness of tone and the humour of his other works are equally present in his examination of Shaw. The book presents a perceptive and far from dated critique of Shaw's philosophy and politics and, through them, the emerging progressive orthodoxy of the 20th century.

The book represents an excellent introduction to Shaw's work and the spirit of the age in which it was created.

Printed in Great Britain
by Amazon.co.uk, Ltd.,
Marston Gate.